SOPHOKLES: *PHILOKTETES*

SOPHOKLES: *PHILOKTETES*

TRANSLATION WITH NOTES, INTRODUCTION, AND INTERPRETIVE ESSAY

SETH L. SCHEIN
UNIVERSITY OF CALIFORNIA, DAVIS

focus an imprint of
Hackett Publishing Company, Inc.
Indianapolis/Cambridge

ISBN 10: 1-58510-086-2
ISBN 13: 978-1-58510-086-6

Cover: Courtesy of The Metropolitan Museum of Art, Fletcher Fund, 1956. (56.171.58) Photograph © 1982 The Metropolitan Museum of Art.

Dio Chrysostom, Discourse 52, *Philoctetes in The Tragedians* by D.A. Russell, from *Ancient Literary Criticism*, ed. D.A. Russell and M. Winterbottom (Oxford, 1972), pp. 504-7. Reprinted by permission of Oxford University Press.

Previously published by Focus Publishing, R. Pullins Co.

Focus an imprint of
Hackett Publishing Company, Inc.
P.O. Box 44937
Indianapolis, Indiana 46244-0937

www.hackettpublishing.com

Printed in the United States of America.

19 18 17 16 15   3 4 5 6

Table of Contents

For Helen Bacon, with whom I first studied *Philoktetes*, and
Daniel Schein, with whom I first saw it performed

Preface

This translation is intended for students, teachers, and general readers who desire a version that is as close to the Greek as I have been able to make it without sacrificing readability. I have tried to preserve or to convey the effects of Sophokles' idioms, imagery, figures of speech, meter, word order, and sentence structure, as well as the combination of a traditional high style with colloquial Attic Greek that is characteristic of all Attic tragedy. Despite some inevitable awkwardness and the impossibility of bringing over into English everything that I see in the Greek, I hope that my version will help readers to achieve an intimate familiarity with the play and its complex meanings.

I have based my translation mainly on the Oxford Classical Text of Sophokles, edited by Hugh Lloyd-Jones and Nigel Wilson,[1] but sometimes I have departed from their text in favor of different manuscript variants or suggestions by modern scholars. I have benefited greatly from the edition and commentary by Sir Richard Jebb and to a lesser extent from the Teubner edition by R.D. Dawe and the commentary by J.C. Kamerbeek.[2] I also have consulted with profit the translations of Hugh Lloyd-Jones, Maria Pia Pattoni, and Judith Affleck.[3] The line numbers in my notes and essays refer to the present translation and occasionally differ by a line or two from the line numbers of the Greek text.

---

[1] H. Lloyd-Jones and N.G. Wilson (edd.), *Sophoclis Fabulae* (Oxford, 1990, corr. 1992)

[2] R.C. Jebb, *Sophocles: the Plays and Fragments. Part IV, The Philoctetes* (2nd edition, Cambrdige, 1898); R.D. Dawe (ed.), *Sophoclis Philoctetes*, (3rd edition, Stuttgart and Leipzig, 1996) [1st edition in *Sophoclis Tragoediae, Tom. II* (Leipzig, 1979), pp. 111-71]; J.C. Kamerbeek, *The Plays of Sophocles. Commentaries, Part VI: The Philoctetes* (Leiden, 1980)

[3] H. Lloyd-Jones, *Sophocles II*, Loeb Classical Library (Cambridge, Mass., 1994), pp. 253-407; M.P. Pattoni, *Sofocle: Trachinie-Filottete*, Introduzione di V. di Benedetto, note di M.S. Mirto, Biblioteca Universale Rizzoli (2nd edition, Milan, 1998), pp. 169-287; J. Affleck, *Sophocles' Philoctetes*, Cambridge Translations from Greek Drama (Cambridge, 2001)

The colleagues, students, and friends with whom I have discussed *Philoktetes* over the years, and whose comments, criticism, and suggestions have improved my understanding of the play, are too numerous to mention. I would, however, like to thank Nancy Felson and Mark Griffith for commenting helpfully on an early draft of the first few hundred lines of the translation; Deborah Roberts and Heather Wood for reading a penultimate version of the translation and notes and for many detailed suggestions that greatly improved them; Carolyn Dewald, Nancy Felson and Heather Wood for helpful criticism of early drafts of the Introduction and Interpretive Essay; Stephen Esposito, editor of the Focus Classical Library, for detailed criticism of the entire manuscript and many helpful suggestions; the anonymous reader for Focus Classical Library for useful comments and recommendations. I am also grateful to Ron Pullins, publisher of the Focus Classical Library, for encouraging this translation and for helpful suggestions in the final stages of preparing; and to Melissa Wood, Production Manager, and Cynthia Zawalich, Copy Editor, at Focus Publishing for their work in transforming that manuscript into a book. Finally, I would like to thank Sherry Crandon for her support and encouragement as I worked on this volume, and I am happy to dedicate it to my teacher, Helen Bacon, with whom I first studied *Philoktetes* in Greek as an undergraduate, and to Daniel Schein, my son, with whom I first saw the play performed.

ACKNOWLEDGMENT

I am grateful to Oxford University Press for permission to reprint, as an Appendix to this volume, D.A. Russell's translation of Dio Chrysostom, *Discourse 52: Philoctetes in the Tragedians*, which originally appeared in *Ancient Literary Criticism*, edited by D.A. Russell and M. Winterbottom (Oxford, 1972), pp. 504-7.

Map of Ancient Greece

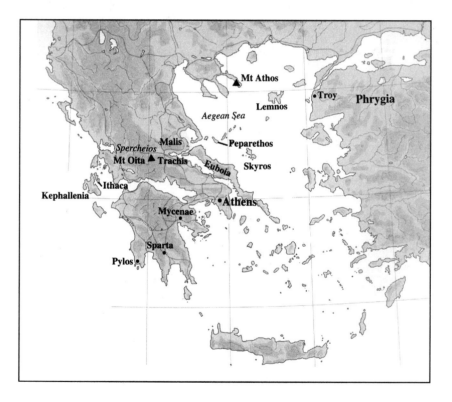

Introduction

According to the traditional chronology, Sophokles was eighty-seven years old when *Philoktetes* was first produced in 409 B.C.E., during the twenty-second year of the Peloponnesian War between Athens and Sparta.[1] Five years later Athens lost its bitter struggle for political and economic hegemony over the hundreds of Greek city-states that co-existed in what today would be considered Greece, the coast of Turkey, southern Italy, and Sicily. The defeat brought to an end the remarkable era of Athenian political, economic, and cultural efflorescence that had begun after the Greek victories in the Persian Wars (490, 480-479), and that included, among other things, the composition and performance of hundreds of tragic dramas at the annual Athenian Spring festival of Dionysos, known as the City Dionysia.[2] Of these hundreds only thirty-two survive, composed by three playwrights: seven by Aischylos (c. 526-456), seven by Sophokles (c. 495-405), and eighteen by Euripides (c. 480-406).[3] The works of these three poets became canonical in the late fifth and fourth centuries, and their use as school texts in later antiquity was probably responsible for the survival of the seven extant plays by Aischylos, the seven by Sophokles, and ten of the eighteen by Euripides. The additional eight plays by Euripides, the titles of which begin with the letters E-K, stem from an alphabetical edition of his works, one part of which survived to be recopied in the Middle Ages. Euripides was extremely popular from the fourth century B.C.E. on, far more so than Aischylos or Sophokles, to judge by the frequent quotations and allu-

---

[1]   All dates are B.C.E. unless otherwise noted.

[2]   The festival was officially part of the cult of Dionysos Eleuthereus, which Athens had imported from Eleutherai, a small town in the region of the border between Attica and Boiotia.

[3]   Counting *Alcestis*, which technically was produced not as a tragedy but in place of a satyr play (see below, p. 5), and not counting *Rhesos*, which, though attributed to Euripides, probably is by some unknown author of the late fifth or early fourth century.

sions to his plays in the works of later ancient authors and the numerous, sometimes extensive fragments of his lost plays that have been discovered since the late nineteenth century on ancient papyri preserved in the sands of Egypt.

The poetic genre in which Aischylos, Sophokles, and Euripides worked, though traditionally called "Greek tragedy," actually was a specifically Athenian phenomenon. One of the most significant changes among students of this genre during the past quarter century has been the increased use of the term "Attic tragedy" rather than Greek tragedy—a term derived from Attica, the peninsula on which Athens is located. Most Attic tragedies were composed for performance in the dramatic competition held annually during the City Dionysia, but there also were competitions at two smaller winter festivals, the Rural Dionysia and (perhaps beginning in the 430s) the Lênaia. The performances at the City Dionysia took place in an open-air theater built into the south slope of the Athenian acropolis. They were attended by audiences of perhaps 15,000-20,000, out of a total population of around 300,000 men, women and children (including citizens, resident aliens, foreigners, and slaves). Undoubtedly citizens—that is, free Athenian males—constituted the great majority of spectators and the main audience to whom the plays were addressed, just as they constituted the entire audience and all the participants in the two other most important institutions of Athenian democracy: the popular assembly that made the laws and decided on Athenian domestic and foreign policy, and the courts of law, where juries numbering hundreds or thousands of jurors provided the ultimate guarantee of the democratic system—the ultimate "power of the people" (in Greek, *dêmokratia*). Women probably could attend the tragic performances—it is not known for certain—but perhaps most who did so were foreign visitors rather than the wives and daughters of citizens.

Athens became a democracy in 508-7, a couple of years after the overthrow of the tyrant Hippias. Hippias had ruled the city since 527 with his brother Hipparchos, succeeding their father Peisistratos in the tyranny he had established about twenty years earlier. Although the city prospered during the generally benevolent reign of Peisistratos and his sons, in later years democratic Athens looked back to the murder of Hipparchos in 514 as one of its foundational moments and celebrated the tyrannicides, Harmodios and Aristogeiton, for having made the city a place where all citizens had equal rights under the law. Increasingly over the next half-century, equality under the law and the freedom of all citizens to serve as jurors, hold a wide variety of military and governmental offices, speak freely in political assemblies, and live as they pleased in their private lives, became the cornerstones of Athenian democracy. The city developed a complex set of political institutions, laws, and practices designed to guarantee these basic civic rights.

Athens flourished as a democracy. In 490 it defeated a Persian army which intended to restore Hippias as tyrant; in 480-79, together with Sparta, it led a coalition of Greek city-states in repulsing a much larger Persian invasion. After these victories in the Persian Wars many members of the coalition formed a new alliance to punish the Persians and liberate the Greek communities on the Aegean islands and along the western and southern coast of Asia Minor. This alliance was known as the Delian League, because its treasury was located on the island of Delos. The Athenian politician and statesmen Aristides made the initial assessment of how many ships and men or how much money each ally should contribute, and Athens took the leading role in the activities of the League. This was partly because it had the largest fleet and was motivated to avenge the burning of the city by the Persians in 480, and partly because Sparta, the only other major Greek military power, was not inclined to do so. Moreover, Athens was ambitious to extend its influence over the cities of the northern and eastern Aegean.

In 454 the League treasury was transferred from Delos to Athens, ostensibly for reasons of security, and from this time on Athens became even more dominant, in effect converting the alliance into an Athenian empire. Athens used the forces of the League to pursue its own military and political ends Whether or not the peace reached with Persia was formally recognized by a treaty in 450-449, soon afterwards Athens appropriated the League's financial resources to fund a massive public works program that included the construction of the Parthenon and several other temples on the Athenian acropolis. Eventually Sparta became fearful of Athenian imperial expansion as a threat to its own empire. After various skirmishes during the 440s and 430s, all-out war between the two cities broke out in 431. This war, known (by its Athenian name) as the Peloponnesian War, lasted on and off for twenty-seven years, until it ended in 404 with the total defeat of the Athenian empire by Sparta and her allies, who now included the Persians.

Between the end of the Persian Wars and the end of the Peloponnesian War, Athenian imperial expansion and wealth were matched by a tremendous cultural efflorescence: this was the great period in which the Parthenon and the other temples, with their magnificent sculptures, were built on the acropolis; Athenian red-figure vase-painting was at its artistic acme; the tragedies of Aischylos, Sophokles, and Euripides were produced at the annual City Dionysia. After 404, democracy was soon restored at Athens, following the eighteen-month reign of terror by the Thirty Tyrants, but there never again was a similar "golden age" of artistic production.[4]

In the era of Athenian imperialism, the City Dionysia, including the tragic competition, was primarily a religious and cultural institution, but it also served to project Athenian wealth, power, and ideology both to the Athenians themselves and to the foreigners in the audiences. These foreigners included the official representatives of Athens' "allies," the member states of the Delian League who paid "tribute" (*phoros*) to Athens each year to support the expenses of the League, in particular the fleet. This annual tribute was publicly displayed in the Theater of Dionysos as part of the festival on the day before the tragic competition began. The festival also included such civic activities as the public award of golden crowns to the city's benefactors and the city's gift of arms and armor to young men whose fathers had been killed in wars against other Greek city-states or "barbarian" (non-Greek) powers, wars in which the Athenians attempted to expand or defend their empire.

In the past two centuries, scholars, critics, and general readers have tended to aestheticize Attic tragedy, frequently viewing it as the purest (because earliest) example of a literary and dramatic form of universal value and meaning. The plays, however, were composed and performed in the specific historical, cultural, and political context of fifth-century Athenian democratic imperialism. Although they were based on traditional, pan-Hellenic mythology, the diction in which the mythical characters spoke was marked by the frequent use of contemporary Athenian legal and political terminology. The dramas must frequently have seemed to their audiences to reflect or to critique specifically Athenian political, social, and cultural institutions and values. It is an open question whether individual plays examined these institutions and values in order to reaffirm and strengthen them, or whether, in the final analysis, the plays were fundamentally subversive. Different members of the audience and different readers may frequently have come to differing judgments about the same works. One thing, however, is certain: the competitions in which the tragedies were performed were genuinely popular events. They combined the appeal in our own time of a parade or a soccer or football game with that of an open air performance of an opera or a play by Shakespeare. Unlike the opera or the Shakespearean play, however, the tragedies, at least in the fifth century, were usually not established "classics" but new representations of well-known myths that

---

[4]   New tragedies continued to be composed in the fourth century, but it is significant that the plays of the great fifth-century dramatists were frequently re-produced in the tragic competitions and in this way attained the status of classics. The democracy lasted until 322, when the Macedonians put an end to it.

resonated meaningfully, and often problematically, with contemporary institutions and ideology.[5] Audiences came to the theater not only to be entertained but prepared to think and to learn something of value.[6]

Remarkably enough, the Athenian state—which means, throughout the fifth century, the mass of the Athenian people—sponsored the tragic competition at public expense. Presumably it did so, at least in part, because the Athenians in the audience were thought to become better, more useful citizens as a result of seeing and hearing the plays. Every year, four plays by each of three poet-playwrights were performed in the tragic competition. These four plays included three tragedies and a satyr-play, so called because the chorus consisted of satyrs whose animality and lewd, boisterous, often drunken behavior provided a kind of comic element.[7] Each playwright was supported by a wealthy citizen, serving as a *chorêgos* ("one who defrays the costs of theatrical production"). The *chorêgos* performed this "public work" (*leitourgia*), imposed on him by the community as a consequence of his wealth, by fully funding all the expenses connected with "the recruiting and maintenance, costuming, and training of the chorus, while the city paid the leading actors and the poets."[8]

One of the nine *archontes*, the leading Athenian administrative officials, was in charge of the City Dionysia. Sometime in the year preceding the festival, he selected, out of all those who desired to enter the

---

[5] There is some evidence of a theatrical revival of Aischylos' *Oresteia*, originally produced in 458, sometime in the late 420s. To judge by the number of times it is quoted, echoed, and alluded to in later fifth-century tragedies, this trilogy must have been familiar to audiences as a kind of "classic," references to which were both recognizable and meaningful.

[6] When a playwright composed and produced a set of plays, he was said to "teach" (*didaskein*) them. The word *didaskalia* ("teaching") was used for the training and rehearsing of a chorus, the tragedies that were produced, and the records later compiled by Aristotle and others of the authors, titles, dates, and relative success of dramas in the tragic competition.

[7] The satyr plays seem often to have had some kind of thematic affinity with one or more of the tragedies in the four-drama sets.

[8] P.E. E[asterling], "tragedy, Greek," *The Oxford Classical Dictionary*, 3rd Edition, ed. S. Hornblower and A. Spawforth (Oxford and New York, 1996), p. 1538. Another kind of *leitourgia* involved paying for a full year the cost of a warship and its crew of about 200. This gives some idea of the kind of expenditure expected of a *chorêgos*, whose conspicuous and unstinting outlay could result in his enhanced symbolic capital, prestige, and political power. Prosecutors and especially defendants in Athenian trials regularly mention their *leitourgiai*, in order to obtain the good will of the citizen jurors.

next tragic competition, the three poets who would "receive a chorus," that is, funding by a *chorêgos*. The criteria of selection are not clear, but perhaps the *archôn* made his choice after hearing the poets read all or part of the plays they hoped to have performed. Like victors in many other competitions in Athens and ancient Greece generally, the winning playwright and *chorêgos* of the tragic competition were awarded a symbolic prize, such as a garland of ivy, by a panel of ten judges. Beginning in 449, there also were prizes for the actors, some of whom were appointed as well as paid by the state, though apparently there were no prizes for the chorus.

The origins and early form of Attic tragedy are unclear, as is the sense of the word "tragedy" itself (*tragôidia*), the verbal elements of which, *trag-* and *ôidia*, suggest "goat" and "song," respectively. Perhaps *tragôidia* originally referred to a song sung by singers at the sacrifice of a goat, or to a goat being a prize in a competition of choral singing. In any event, what we call an Attic tragedy was simply a poetic drama produced in the tragic competition during the City Dionysia. These tragedies were by no means always "tragic" in later senses of the word: their plots did not necessarily involve a fall from high estate to low degree, nor did they have to end unhappily. Many Attic tragedies, including Aischylos' *Oresteia*, Euripides' *Alkestis, Ion, Helen*, and *Iphigeneia among the Taurians*, and Sophokles' *Philoktetes* and *Oidipous at Kolonos*, have happy endings, though in most cases these endings are somehow qualified and the plays are, to some degree, open-ended. In this respect, these tragedies resemble certain plays by Shakespeare, especially the romances and "problem comedies," the happy endings of which are marked by irony and ambivalence and "[do] not exhaust the energies of the drama."[9] It is at least as accurate and fruitful to think of *Philoktetes* as a romance as it is to consider it a tragedy in any modern sense of the word.[10]

Despite the traditional story that a certain Thespis first composed and produced a tragedy sometime between 535 and 533, during the reign of the tyrant Peisistratos, it is possible that the tragic competition was initiated after Athens became a democracy in 508-7. At the very least, tragedy became a far more important literary form and civic institution under the democracy and remained so throughout the fifth century. Aristotle says (*Poetics* 4.1449a9-11) that tragedy developed by improvisation from an earlier form of choral poetry known as the dithyramb, when the

---

[9] Stephen Orgel, "Introduction," *The Tempest, The Oxford Shakespeare* (Oxford and New York, 1987), p. 55

[10] See Carola Greengard, *Theatre in Crisis: Sophocles' Reconstruction of Genre and Politics in Philoctetes* (Amsterdam, 1987).

leader of the chorus (Thespis?) separated himself from the group and in some way engaged in dialogue with it, thus transforming himself into an actor (*hypokritês*, "one who interprets" or, perhaps, "one who responds"). Aristotle credits Aischylos with reducing the choral part and increasing the number of actors from one to two, and he says that Sophokles added a third actor and introduced painted scenery (4.1449a16-19). The plays of Aischylos contain proportionally more choral song than those of Sophokles and Euripides, which might support the notion that the genre originated in choral performance and gradually came to include more dialogue composed in meter that was spoken rather than sung.[11]

Tragedy and comedy are the only genres of ancient Greek poetry that juxtapose spoken and sung verse. This highly unusual juxtaposition of meters suggests that tragedy, like comedy, was a deliberately invented genre rather than the product of a gradual development within a poetic tradition. On the other hand, tragedy employs the meters and dialects traditionally appropriate to spoken and sung verse in other genres of Greek poetry. For example, the choral songs (or odes) are composed in, or at least show distinctive features of, Doric, the Greek dialect that is standard in choral poetry, regardless of whether the poet or his audience were native Doric speakers. Similarly, the language of dialogue is Attic with an admixture of Ionic, the main dialect used in earlier "spoken" verse, including both traditional heroic epic and the iambic trimeter poems of such late seventh- and early sixth-century authors as Archilochos, Semonides, and Solon.

Iambic trimeter is the main meter of tragic dialogue between individuals, though occasionally, for some special effect, the poets also employ trochaic tetrameter catalectic, which Aristotle (Poetics 4.1449a21-2) says was the earliest spoken meter used in tragedy. The speeches and dialogue composed in iambic trimeter may have been less powerful, metrically and musically, than the choral songs; nevertheless, the varying style and rhetoric of trimeter verse enabled the actors to portray and interpret individual characters' thoughts and feelings in ways that would have affected the audiences both intellectually and emotionally. This must

---

11   Meter (from the Greek word *metron*, "measure") is the measured arrangement of words in poetry. Such an arrangement usually involves a more or less fixed number of syllables per line, as well as the patterned alternation of syllables with contrasting acoustic phenomena—for example, stressed and unstressed syllables in English, odd and even tones in Chinese, or "heavy" and "light" syllables in ancient Greek. The word "meter" is also used of particular arrangements of words as determined by the number of metrical units in a line: for example, iambic pentameter (a line of five iambic units) in English or iambic trimeter (a line of three iambic units) in Greek.

have been especially true in sub-genres such as the messenger speech, with its vivid narration of violent and shocking events that happened offstage; the rhetorical agôn ("formal debate"), with its symmetrically paired speeches presenting conflicting and often hostile points of view; and stichomythia ("speaking in individual lines"), with its verbal fencing in single lines spoken alternatively by different characters.

Tragic choruses seem to have consisted originally of twelve and later of fifteen members, who sang and danced to the accompaniment of a flute in the *orchêstra*, the "circular dancing area" from which the stone seats of the *theatron* (amphitheater) radiated outward and upward.[12] Relatively early in a play, they entered the *orchêstra* by one or both of two side passageways called *eisodoi* (or *parodoi*), singing their entry song, the *parodos*. It is uncertain whether the choral dances were in some way representational or whether they consisted mainly of metaphorical or abstract movements and gestures. Sometimes the name of a meter may give an indication: for example, the meter most associated with outbursts of intense emotion is called "dochmiac," a name that seems to derive from a word meaning "sideways" (or "slantwise") and might suggest that the members of the chorus threw themselves sideways when they danced songs composed in this meter. In most cases, however, the names of the meters offer no clue as to the nature of the choral movement. It is difficult, too, to link particular meters with particular kinds of content, though in some plays repeated metrical motifs or patterns seem to be associated with particular themes or ideas. For example, in *Philoktetes* it appears that when the Choros are actively assisting or prompting Neoptolemos to betray Philoktetes, they shift from from one kind of meter known as "Aeolic" to another called "iambo-trochaic." Many of the meters used in tragic choral song occur elsewhere in Greek literature in ritual contexts and may give a "ritual dimension" to the scenes in which they occur.[13]

The choral songs of Attic tragedy, like most other Greek choral poetry, are usually organized stanzaically in one or more sequences of *strophê* and *antistrophê*. These words, which literally mean "turn" and "counterturn," were originally dance terms and probably referred to physical movements in the choral dance. In metrical terms, a given *strophê* and *antistrophê* are said to "correspond": that is, in both *strophê* and *antistrophê* the sequence, or patterned alternation, of "heavy" and "light" syllables is identical, regardless of where the words containing

---

[12]   The word *theatron* also could mean the spectators (*theatai*) considered as a collective body or aggregate.

[13]   E[asterling], "tragedy, Greek," p. 1540.

these syllables end and what they mean. Not only was the pattern of syllabic quantity in a corresponding *strophê* and *antistrophê* identical, but presumably the music and choreography also were the same—or if there were differences, they were perceptible against the background of the identical metrical pattern. The need for metrical corresponsion between *strophê* and *antistrophê* may at times have been oppressive, but

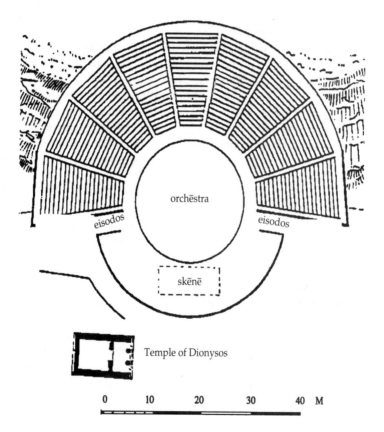

A reconstruction of the theater of Dionysos in Athens during the second half of the fifth century BCE. (Based on the sketch by J. Travlos, Pictorial Dictionary of Ancient Athens [London 1971] 540.)

like all such formal constraints it also would have enabled the poets to express or heighten certain types of meaning more easily and effectively than in less formally patterned verse.[14]

All choruses in Greek poetry and society, including tragic choruses, sang in a communal voice with communal authority.[15] In any given play, the Choros has a specific, consistent dramatic identity (men or women, young or old, of a particular community). When, in the person of its leader, the Choros engages in dialogue or takes part in the dramatic action, it expresses ideas, attitudes, and values shaped by and expressive of this identity. Its songs, however, can move from specific details of dramatic action to generalizations about the human condition and the divine order of the cosmos. These songs also can move forward or backward in time, making connections between present, past, and future actions and sufferings, and inviting audiences to reflect on the meaning of these actions and sufferings in a broader political, social, or religious context. Although the Chorus is not simply an ideal version of the audience in the theater, the audience must sometimes have identified with the Chorus as a communal voice. Quite often choral reflections either heighten audience tensions or else relieve them by offering consolation or providing insight into apparently incomprehensible or uncontrollable dramatic actions and sufferings. On occasion, choral song can even transform the gods, who seem to act arbitrarily or unjustly, into sources or guarantors of social justice and cosmic order.

Sometimes there is an exchange in which an actor "speaks" in the iambic trimeter of dialogue and the Chorus sings (and presumably dances) its response; other times the Chorus and one of the actors address one another in song; occasionally an actor sings an extended monody—a kind of aria—in a meter usually reserved for choral song. Whenever an actor breaks into song, the moment is highly emotional, as in *Philoktetes* 1081-1217, when the Chorus try to persuade Philoktetes to leave the island and accompany them to Troy and he persists in his refusal to do so.

In addition to the meters of dialogue and choral song, Attic tragedy also employs anapestic meter. This is a kind of spoken or chanted verse in the same dialect as the dialogue, which is especially common when characters are entering, exiting, or moving around on the stage. Sometimes anapests alternate or are mixed with choral song, and in such

---

14   Occasionally a *strophê* and *antistrophê* are followed by an *epôdê*, a noncorresponding metrical sequence different from but related to that of the *strophê* and *antistrophê*.

15   See Helen H. Bacon, "The Chorus in Greek Life and Drama," *Arion*, 3rd Series, 3 (1994-95), pp. 6-25.

cases they use the ordinary lyric dialect and probably were sung. Even in this passage, however, the clear contrast between the corresponding strophes and antistrophes sung by the Chorus and Neoptolemos' sung anapests marks the difference in attitude with which each awaits the coming of Philoktetes.

Attic tragedy never allowed more than three speaking actors "on stage" at the same time, though there were plenty of silent characters. It was common for the same actor to play two or more roles in the course of a play. (In *Philoktetes*, for example, a single actor played Odysseus, the sailor disguised as a merchant captain, and Herakles.) The actors entered and exited by the same side passageways as the chorus. Although they must have sometimes interacted with the chorus in the *orchêstra*, for the most part they probably stood on a slightly raised wooden platform just behind it and just in front of a stage building (*skênê*), which could be painted as a backdrop representing a palace, a temple, or some other interior space, such as the cave in which Philoktetes dwells. An actor could enter this interior space through a door in the stage building, and in some cases could appear on its roof or above it in a kind of crane. This was most often the case in so-called *deus ex machina* ("god out of the machine") endings, like that in *Philoktetes* (1409 ff.).

The actors were all male, even those who played the female parts. (*Philoktetes* is the only extant Attic tragedy with no female character.) They were masked, lavishly costumed, and probably relied heavily on formulaic gestures and movements. Nevertheless, even through their masks, the most important element of their acting, which enabled them to reach and to move their extremely large and sometimes boisterous audiences, was their vocal projection and linguistic expressiveness, enhanced by the theater's superb acoustics.

   * * * *

Little is known for certain about the life of Sophokles. The late biography that has come down in the manuscripts of the plays, like all ancient Greek lives of poets, does not aim at what we might call factual accuracy. Rather it constructs a "life" and tells stories that were thought to be appropriate or in character for the person who wrote the plays.[16] Some anecdotes are preserved in the meager fragments of the memoir by Ion of Chios, another fifth-century tragic playwright, of his conversations with Sophokles. Other stories survive in diverse works by Plato, Aristotle, and Plutarch; in the life of Euripides by the third-

---

[16] There is a translation of the *Life of Sophocles* in M. Lefkowitz, *The Lives of the Greek Poets* (Baltimore and London, 1981), pp. 160-63, with discussion on pp. 66-74.

century author Satyros; in ancient *scholia* (marginal comments) in the manuscripts of various plays by Euripides and Aristophanes; and on the so-called *Marmor Parium (Parian Marble)*, an inscribed marble stele found on the island of Paros, which contains a chronological listing (sometimes inaccurate) of various events in political, military, religious, and literary history down to 264-3, and which probably was composed not long after that date.

What seems certain is that Sophokles had an exceptionally long and successful career in the theater. Born about 496, he came of age in the decades when Athens successfully resisted the Persian invasions of 490 and 480-79 and dominated the "Delian League." Sophokles is reported to have won the tragic competion in 468, when he competed in it for the first time. His final appearance was in 406, shortly before his death, when he is said to have dressed his chorus and actors in mourning to honor Euripides, of whose death he had just learned. His latest extant play, *Oidipous at Kolonos*, was probably composed during the last year of his life; it was produced posthumously in 401.

Over 120 plays were attributed to Sophokles in later antiquity, including about 90 tragedies and 30 satyr plays. This suggests that he competed in the City Dionysia approximately 30 times, or roughly every other year. He is variously said to have won 18 or 20 or 24 victories and never to have placed worse than second. He competed against Aischylos until the latter's death in 456 and against Euripides from about 455 on. The chronology of the seven extant plays is uncertain. There is external evidence that *Philoktetes* was produced in 409 when Sophokles was 87 years old, and that *Oidipous at Kolonos* was produced posthumously in 401, but no such evidence exists by which to date the other five plays. *Elektra*, which has thematic and dramaturgical affinities with *Philoktetes*, probably was composed between 415 and 410, and *Oidipous the King* around 425. *Antigone* is conventionally dated to about 442, on the strength of a story that Sophocles was chosen as one of the ten Athenian generals for the war against Samos in 441-40 because of the success of the play.[17] *Antigone* has structural affinities with *Ajax* and *The Women of Trachis*, which usually are considered the earliest of the extant plays and may date from the 450s or 440s. *The Women of Trachis*, however, may have been composed sometime in the 420s, given its thematic similarities to *Oidipous the King*, especially its emphasis on "learning too late" the true meaning of oracles and the impossibility of escaping their predictions.

---

[17]   Euripides is reported in the *Marmor Parium* to have won first prize for the first time in the competition of 441.

Sophocles is quoted by Plutarch, "Progress in Virtue," 7.79B, as having described his development in the following terms: "having got through the stages of playing with Aeschylean grandiloquence and then with the displeasing and artificial element in my own manner of elaborating my theme, now in the third stage I am changing to the kind of style that is most expressive of character and best" (tr. H. Lloyd-Jones). It is not known whether Sophokles actually made this comment, or if so, when. If his chronological development can be divided into three stages, it is likely that all the extant plays belong to the third. Certainly they all show a fundamental consistency in style and characterization, despite differences from play to play.

Sophokles also is reported (by Aristotle, *Poetics* 25.1460b33-34) to have said that he presented men "as they ought to be" (or "as they ought to be presented") and Euripides "as they are." Whatever this may mean, Sophokles' "presentation" of character in the extant plays seems consistent, though some characters in his latest works more fully reflect the rhetoric and (a)moral relativism of the Sophistic movement that made itself felt in Athens with increasing force during the final third of the fifth century. Because the Sophists primarily taught skills of rhetorical persuasion, they were especially popular and influential at Athens, where the institutions of democracy put a premium on the ability of individual speakers to persuade large audiences to do what they wanted, and where even ordinary citizens had a relatively sophisticated understanding of, and weakness for, sophistic rhetorical techniques. Sophokles may seem less flamboyantly sophistic than Euripides, but the influence on him of the sophists is especially clear in the long speeches in which characters formally debate one another. Sophokles' opinion of the Sophistic movement is uncertain, but in the later plays at least, he negatively characterizes such sophistically tinged figures as Orestes in *Elektra* and Odysseus in *Philoktetes* as amoral pragmatists and self-aggrandizing opportunists.[18]

It is unlikely that Sophokles was really chosen general because of the success of *Antigone*, but the story does call attention to a significant difference between Sophokles, on the one hand, and Aischylos and Euripides, on the other. Of the three playwrights, only Sophokles is said to have held public office in the Athenian democracy. He served

---

[18]   The strongly negative representations of the Sophists in the dialogues of Plato (followed generally by Aristotle) gave the sophists a bad reputation, which for the most part has persisted to the present day. For more favorable evaluations, see W.K.C. Guthrie, "The World of the Sophists," *A History of Greek Philosophy*, Vol. 3 (Cambridge 1969), pp. 1-319; G.B. Kerferd, *The Sophistic Movement* (Cambridge 1981).

as *Hellênotamias* ("treasurer") of the Delian League in 443-42, more than a decade after its treasury had been transferred from Delos to Athens. As *Hellênotamias*, Sophokles would have helped to handle the annual tribute paid to Athens by its "allies"; as general in the campaign against Samos he helped to control and chastise a rebellious ally. In both these capacities, Sophokles was associated with the imperialistic policies of Perikles, the politician/statesman who dominated the Athenian democracy from about 460 to his death in 429, and who himself served as the leading general during the Samian War. Long after the death of Perikles, according to Aristotle (*Rhetoric* III.1419a25-30), Sophokles, at the age of 85 or 86, served as one of the ten special "advisers" (*probouloi*) appointed to deal with the political crisis following the failure in 413 of the Athenian attempt to conquer Sicily. He is reported to have endorsed an oligarchical constitution at this time, "because there was nothing else better." Sophokles is also said to have served as priest of a cult-hero called Halon, who was somehow associated with healing, and to have temporarily received into his house the cult serpent of the healer-god Asklepios, when this cult was imported to Athens around 420. Perhaps these stories account for the intriguing report in the *Life* that after his death, Sophocles was himself worshipped posthumously as the cult-hero Dexion, "the receiver."

It is unclear whether or not this report is true. For the Greeks, hero cults provided a kind of posthumous immortality for mortals whose actions and achievements during their lifetimes were so extraordinary that they seemed to transcend normal human limits. Most cult heroes were figures out of the mythological past--one thinks of Sophocles' Ajax, Antigone, Elektra, and Oidipous--though there is evidence too for the heroization in the fifth century of well known individuals, such as the Spartan general Brasidas, whose achievements were considered particularly outstanding and valuable to their communities. Those who became "heroes," especially the traditional, mythological figures, might have seemed repellent, even monstrous, during their lifetimes. After death, however, the power manifested in a hero's actions was worshipped in a chthonic cult and, so to speak, socially harnessed at the site of the grave, where the hero could exert beneficent power on behalf of the local community of worshippers. There certainly was a cult in Athens of a hero named Dexion, but if Sophokles was worshipped under this name, he would be the only adult known to have been worshipped as a hero with a name different from his own.

Whether or not Sophokles was worshipped as Dexion, the story is appropriate to him not only because, in the plot of his final play, *Oidipous at Kolonos*, Oidipous becomes a hero, but because nearly all his extant dramas include characters who are known to have been worshipped in actual hero cults. In *Ajax*, the tomb of Ajax, who in the fifth century was one of the ten heroes for whom the Athenian tribes were named,[19] is virtually consecrated by the Chorus as a site of power and a place of future worship.[20] Sophokles' tragedies repeatedly explore the heroic identity of characters who are more than human in their power, integrity, and intransigent refusal to compromise their moral standards, but all-too-human in their mortal misperception of the nature of reality and their place in the universe, and in the suffering and death that this misperception and their eventual (self-)recognition entail for themselves, their families, and their communities.[21]

This (self-)recognition often involves a changed sense of the connections and relationships between human beings and the gods. In all of Sophokles' extant plays divinity is present to human beings through oracles, prophecies, and dreams. It also can be seen in such extraordinary phenomena as the Theban plague in *Oidipous the King* and the incurable wound of Philoktetes. Humans frequently address prayers to the gods—sometimes, as in *Oidipous the King* and *Elektra*, directly to their cult statues—and try to act in accordance with what they consider to be divine laws, standards, and intentions. Nevertheless, they consistently misunderstand their relationship to divinity: they frequently misinterpret oracles and dreams, disbelieve authoritative prophecies, and generally learn too late, if at all, the actual meanings of divine communications, usually after they have destroyed themselves and others through misguided actions. If human actions, sufferings, and manifestations of divinity ultimately cohere and make sense, they do so only in retrospect, never in time to avert catastrophe.

Philoktetes is exceptional in that these things never do cohere and make sense. The meaning of the divine communications—Helenos'

---

19 When the Athenian democracy was created in 508-7, the political reformer Kleisthenes divided the Athenian population into ten groups called tribes (*phylai*), each of which was comprised of a third (*trittys*) from the city, a third from the shore, and a third from the inland area. The idea was to reduce the power of regional interests to threaten the city-state as a whole. The tribes became the organizational units from which equal numbers of citizens were drawn to fill a variety of political, military, and judicial offices and activities and for athletic and choral competitions at various festivals. Each tribe was named for a traditional hero of myth or history, and each had its own officials and religious centers.

20 Cf. A. Henrichs, "The Tomb of Aias and the Prospect of Hero Cult in Sophocles' *Ajax*," *Classical Antiquity* 12 (1993), pp. 165-80, esp. 170.

21 See B.M.W. Knox, *The Heroic Temper: Studies in Sophoclean Tragedy* (Berkeley and Los Angeles, 1964).

prophecy (whatever its actual terms), Philoktetes' snakebite, Herakles' final intervention *ex machina*—never becomes clear, and it remains uncertain what the gods truly intend or even whether there is such a thing as the "truth" of their intentions. Even in the tragedies that seem to end with everything falling into place, Sophokles challenges his audiences and readers to interpret ethically this apparent coherence—to ponder, for example, the statement in the final line of *The Women of Trachis* that "there is none of this that is not Zeus"; to make sense of the workings of Eros and Dionysos in *Antigone* or of Apollo and the Furies in *Elektra* and the two *Oidipous* plays. Generally speaking, the gods remain beyond good and evil; morality and moral agency reside in the human characters, who can transcend the limitations of the human condition by their ethically meaningful choices and actions.

These choices and actions take place in the midst of the conflicts, conscious and unconscious, that are a basic feature of Sophoklean tragedy. There are intra-familial conflicts between men and women, parents and children; intrasocietal conflicts between individuals and their communities; intersocietal conflicts, most notably between Athens and Thebes in *Oidipous at Kolonos*. In addition, intensely moving intrapsychic conflicts afflict the minds of the main characters, as they debate appropriate courses of action, resist the temptation to be false to their fundamental values, and affirm their heroic identities.

The rhythm of Sophoklean tragedy, as of Attic tragedy generally, involves the alternation of scenes of dialogue with choral songs. Usually a Sophoklean choral song begins with language that refers or responds, explicitly or implicitly, to something that has just happened or just been said in the action or dialogue. Then the song may move backward in time to describe, allude to, narrate, or reflect upon a traditional myth, illustrating either some notable example of human action or suffering relevant to the issues of the play or the working of the gods in relation to mortals. Undoubtedly, the dance and music that are no longer extant would have made these songs even more powerful emotionally than they are nowadays when read or spoken in performance. Like the songs in Shakespeare's plays, Sophokles' choral songs condense the imagery and ideas of the dramas and call attention to their fundamental themes and interpretive problems.

These songs, like those by Aischylos and Euripides, also might be said, in modern terms, to divide the plays into "acts," since they usually are preceded by the exits and followed by the entrances of individual characters. A typical Sophoclean tragedy might have four or even five choral songs in addition to the *parodos*. *Philoktetes* is exceptional in having, in addition to the *parodos*, only two relatively brief songs (676-729; 828-

64, interrupted by Neoptolemos at 839-42), as well as two other short outbursts that correspond metrically as *strophê* and *antistrophê* (391-402, 507-18) and the long lyric exchange between Philoktetes and the Chorus (1081-1217). The relative paucity of choral song in *Philoktetes* is the counterpart to the Chorus' active participation in Odysseus' intrigue and apparent exclusion from the human and divine solidarities with which the play ends. This Chorus provide no detached, "choral" voice with which members of the audience can associate themselves or make a point of departure for their own thoughts. This lack of a choral voice contributes to the play's notable and problematic lack of any consolatory, enlightening, or uplifting perspective on its own events and values.

The Sophoklean iambic trimeter is far more flexible and varied than the Aeschylean and Euripidean trimeters, and more attuned to developments in the dramatic action. For example, there is more frequent, and more effective, enjambment, where the thought flows over the end of one line to the beginning of the next with no syntactic break; more disappointment of expected word-end and more "resolution" (two "light" syllables instead of one "heavy" syllable") at particular positions in the line. This distinctive metrical flexibility and variety contribute to dramatic characterization and help to call attention to thematically significant words and ideas. Frequently the conflicts between characters are represented rhetorically not only in extended, formal debates, but in intense exchanges of a few lines or single lines (*stichomythia*), with the most impassioned moments marked by the division of individual lines between two speakers (*antilabê*). *Antilabê* can also convey an unexpected shock or surprise, as when Odysseus unexpectedly enters in the midst of *Philoktetes* 974.

There has been a tendency since antiquity to reduce the power and complexity of Sophoklean drama by pat, oversimplistic critical formulations, for example, "most Homeric," or "He saw life steadily and he saw it whole." Such formulations may have some truth in them, but they err in treating the plays as if they were calm, balanced, and serene, and in this way veil their true dramatic force.[22] Sometimes Sophoklean tragedy has been seen, by both professional scholars and general readers, as "classical" in comparison to the "archaic" works of Aischylos and the "modern" or "counter-classical" dramas of Euripides. If "classical" involves the notion of serving as a standard or model, the tendency to view Sophoklean tragedy in this way probably was intensified by Hegel's idealization of *Antigone* as the Attic tragedy par excellence, which helped

---

[22]   Cf. Aristophanes' characterization of Sophocles as *eukolos* ("relaxed" or "easy going") in *Frogs* 82 .

to make it the most widely read and performed ancient Greek drama during the nineteenth century.[23] Similarly, when Freud, in *The Interpretation of Dreams*, drew on his (mis)understanding of *Oidipous the King* to set forth his theory of the Oedipus complex for the first time,[24] he made that play paradigmatic for twentieth-century students of Attic tragedy, in effect providing a modern version of Aristotle's argument that its plot is particularly successful because of the emotional effect (on audiences and readers) of its plausible and coincident scenes of recognition and reversal (*Poetics* 11.1452a22-b8).

Sophoklean tragedy, however, is much more turbulent and problematic that any one-dimensional, universalizing interpretation might suggest. When read attentively in light of their fifth-century Athenian cultural context, the plays are charged with a variety of emotional, intellectual, and ethical meanings. These meanings are still available to us today, not least because, for better and worse, we have inherited from fifth-century Athens many of our fundamental institutions and values, and we still wrestle with similar emotional, intellectual, and ethical conflicts and problems.

---

[23]   Cf. G. Steiner, *Antigones* (Oxford, 1984), pp. 19-42.

[24]   See B.M.W. Knox, *Oedipus at Thebes* (New Haven and London, 1957; reprinted 1966), pp. 3-5.

Philoktetes

DRAMATIS PERSONAE

ODYSSEUS, a Greek leader at Troy
NEOPTOLEMOS, the son of Achilles
CHORUS OF NEOPTOLEMOS' SAILORS
SAILOR (as Lookout and Merchant Captain)
PHILOKTETES, a Greek leader abandoned on Lemnos
HERAKLES, a deified hero

*(Setting: a deserted spot on the northeast coast of the uninhabited island,
Lemnos, near Mt. Hermaion. A cave opens into a steep cliff that rises above
the shore. Odysseus and Neoptolemos enter from the audience's left, followed
by a Sailor.)*

ODYSSEUS

This is the shore of Lemnos, a land circled by the sea;
it's uninhabited, and no mortal sets foot on it.[1]
Here, Neoptolemos, you who are sprung from the mightiest
    of Greek
fathers, true-bred son of Achilles—here I once abandoned
the son of Poias from Malis,[2] like a new-born child.   5

---

[1] *Lemnos*: an island with an area of 183 square miles in the northern Aegean
Sea, about equidistant from Troy (to the east) and Mt. Athos (to the
west). That Lemnos is uninhabited is a radical innovation on the part of
Sophokles. In the *Iliad* the island is called "well-settled" (21.40), and its
King Eunêos engages in trade with the Greek army (7.467-71). Ironically,
the "uninhabited" island that "no mortal sets foot on" (*brotois astiptos*) will
turn out to be inhabited by the distinctive "footstep" (*stibos*) of Philoktetes
(158, 163, 206); the same word is used elsewhere in the play of human
tracks, paths, or footfalls, e.g. 29, 48, 487.

[2] *Malis*: a region on the east coast of mainland Greece, opposite the northwest

I was following the kings' orders: his foot was ulcerous
and kept dripping from the disease that was eating through it;
we couldn't put our hands to a libation or sacrifice
in peace and quiet: each time he would fill the whole camp
with inauspicious, savage cries,   10
shouting and groaning. But why should I go on speaking
of these things? We have no time for long speeches.
He may learn that I've come, and I'll waste the whole
clever plan by which I expect to catch him right away.[3]
Your task from now on is to serve me and, in particular,   15
to scout out where there's a two-mouthed cave nearby--
the sort where in winter there are two places
to sit in the sun's warmth, and in summer
a cool breeze sends sleep through a grotto open at both ends.
A little below, on the left, you may see a fresh-water spring   20
welling up, if it is still there and still running.
Don't make a sound, but go and signal me if he still keeps to
this same place, or if he happens to be somewhere else,
so you may hear the rest of what I have to say,
and I may explain things, and a joint action may proceed from us
  both.[4]   25

---

coast of Euboia, a long island running NW to SE. Poias, the King of Malis
and father of Philoktetes, probably would have been known to Sophokles'
original audience as one of the Argonauts (cf. [Apollodorus], *The Library*,
I.9.16, 26), and they would have understood "the son of Poias" to be
Philoktetes. In any case, Odysseus' reference to abandoning him on Lemnos
because of his diseased foot would have made his identity completely clear.
(Philoktetes is called by his own name only six times in the play: 55, 101,
263, 432, 575, 1261.)

3   *"clever plan"*: *sophisma*. Here as elsewhere in the Prologue, Odysseus uses
    a word that associates him with the fifth-century Sophistic movement
    (see above, Introduction, p. 13). Cf. 77: "be clever," *sophisthênai*; 80:
    "contrive," *technasthai*; 119: "clever," *sophos*; 131: "what is advantageous,"
    ta sumpheronta.

4   In ancient Greek, in addition to the singular and plural, there was a
    separate "dual" number used of two persons or things which, by nature
    or association, belong together and form an equal pair. Here, as at the end
    of the Prologue (133), Odysseus uses a "dual" form persuasively to make
    Neoptolemos seem to be on an equal footing with himself. Other significant
    uses of the dual occur at 533, 1079, and 1436.

NEOPTOLEMOS
King Odysseus, the task you speak of is not far off:
I think I see the sort of cave you mentioned.

ODYSSEUS
Up above, or below? I don't have a clear picture.

NEOPTOLEMOS
Here above, and there's not a sound of a footstep.

ODYSSEUS
See if he happens to be asleep, taking shelter inside.   30

NEOPTOLEMOS
I see an empty dwelling, with no one there.

ODYSSEUS
Is there no provision within that would make it a home?

NEOPTOLEMOS
Yes, a pressed down bed of leaves, as if someone were camping
    inside.

ODYSSEUS
Everything else is empty? There's nothing under the roof?

NEOPTOLEMOS
Just a cup made from a piece of wood, the contrivance of some   35
poor craftsman, and also this kindling for starting a fire.

ODYSSEUS
This treasure you're describing is his.

NEOPTOLEMOS
Aha! Yes, there are these other things too drying in the sun,
rags filled with the matter from some disgusting disease.

ODYSSEUS
Clearly the man dwells in this place,   40
and he's somewhere not far off. For how could he
go far, a man whose foot is sick with an old disease?
No, either he's gone out to bring home something to feed on,[5]
or he knows of some herb that dulls the pain.
Send the man who is with you as a lookout,   45

---

[5] *"something to feed on"*: here and in 163 Odysseus uses a word that might
(disrespectfully) suggest an animal feeding rather than a human being.

so he won't fall on me unexpectedly. He would rather
catch me than take all the other Argives.

NEOPTOLEMOS
All right, the man is going and the footpath will be guarded.
If there's anything else you want, speak again and tell me.

ODYSSEUS
Son of Achilles, you must be noble   50
in what you've come for, not only physically,
but if you hear something new that you haven't heard previously,
you must be of service, since you're here as a servant.

NEOPTOLEMOS
What, then, do you command?[6]

ODYSSEUS
                                        You must, by speaking,
see that you deceive Philoktetes' mind with your words.[7]   55
When he asks who you are and where you've come from,
say, "The son of Achilles"; in this there must be no deception;
you're sailing home, after conceiving a great hatred
for the Achaians and leaving their naval expedition—
the Achaians who sent for you with prayers to come from home,   60
considering this their only means of sacking Troy,
but when you had come, did not think you worthy of the arms of
   Achilles
and wouldn't give them to you when you asked for them as their
   proper lord
and master, but instead handed them over to Odysseus! Say as
   much as
you want against us, the most extreme of extreme evils.   65
You won't cause me any pain by this, but if you don't
do it, you'll cast sorrow on all the Argives.

---

6   The division of a line between two speakers (*antilabê*) marks a special
     urgency or intensity of feeling that, as it were, cannot be bound within
     normal metrical constraints. Cf. 201, 210, 732, 736, 753-9, 810-17, 974, 981,
     985, 994, 1001, 1174, 1182, 1185, 1204, 1210, 1211, 1296, 1302, 1402-7.

7   *deceive Philoktetes' mind"* : *psuchên...ekklepseis*. These words also might be
     translated, "steal Philoktetes' life." Odysseus' syntax in the Greek of 54-55
     is unusual and somewhat awkward. Like the three "must"s in 50, 53, and
     54, it is both a sign of his difficulty in telling the "noble" son of Achilles
     that he must lie and a rhetorical tactic to overcome this difficulty.

For if this man's bow shall not be taken,
it's impossible for you to sack the plain of Dardanos.[8]
Now understand why contact with this man is impossible   70
for me but safe and trustworthy for you:
you have set sail bound by oath to no man
and on no compulsion,[9] nor were you part of the first expedition,
but I can deny none of these things.
So if he catches sight of me while master of his bow,   75
I am lost, and by association I will destroy you as well.
No, this is just the thing in which you must be clever, so you
may become the thief of the invincible weapons.
I know well, my son, that by nature you were not born
to contrive such things or utter such evils.   80
Since, however, the possession of victory is something sweet to gain,
bring yourself to do it; we'll appear to be just on another occasion.
Give yourself to me now for a brief portion of a day
for something shameful, and then for the rest of time
be called the most pious of all mortals.[10]   85

NEOPTOLEMOS
Son of Laertes, the words that I feel pain on hearing
are those I also hate to put into practice;
I was born to do nothing by evil contrivance—
neither I myself nor, as they say, the one who sired me.
But I'm ready to take the man by force   90
instead of deceit: on one foot he won't
by force get the best of us who are so many.
I've been sent to cooperate with you, and I hesitate
to be called a traitor. Yet I prefer, O king, to fail
by doing well rather than to conquer by evil means.   95

ODYSSEUS
Son of a brave and noble father, when I was young

---

8   *"the plain of Dardanos"*: the plain of Troy. Dardanos was an ancestor of the
     Trojan king, Priam.

9   *"bound by oath...on no compulsion"*: a reference to the oath sworn by
     Helen's suitors to her father, Tyndareus, that they would come to the aid
     of whomever she might choose for her husband, should she be seduced or
     abducted by another man (as she later was by Paris).

10   *"be called the most pious"*: Odysseus implies that Neoptolemos would be
     acting impiously, if he "give[s] [him]self" to Odysseus.

I too once had an idle tongue and an active hand.
But now, as I go forth to the test, I see that among mortals
it's speech, not action, that leads the way in all things.[11]

NEOPTOLEMOS
What else, then, are you commanding me, except to tell lies?   100

ODYSSEUS
I'm telling you to take Philoktetes by deceit.

NEOPTOLEMOS
Why must I bring him by deceit rather than by persuading him?

ODYSSEUS
He will not be persuaded, and you could not take him by force.

NEOPTOLEMOS
Does some terrible strength give him such confidence?

ODYSSEUS
Yes, he has inescapable arrows that send forth death.   105

NEOPTOLEMOS
Then one cannot dare even to approach the man?

ODYSSEUS
No, unless you take him by deceit, as I'm telling you.

NEOPTOLEMOS
You don't, then, consider telling lies to be shameful?

ODYSSEUS
No, I don't, if the lie brings salvation.

NEOPTOLEMOS
With what face will anyone bring himself to say these things out
loud?   110

ODYSSEUS
When you do something for profit, it's not appropriate to hesitate.

---

[11]   In Greek, the same word, *glôssa*, means both "tongue" and "speech." A
scholiast (ancient commentator) on 99 suggests that in 96-99 Sophokles
"slanders" contemporary Athenian political leaders, on whom he models
Odysseus (see Note on 134) Cf. 407-9. In Euripides' *The Trojan Women* (415
B.C.E.), Hekabe refers to Odysseus' "twofold tongue," with which "he twists
everything from that side to this / and then back again to that, / making
what was formerly loved unloved" (285-88).

NEOPTOLEMOS

What profit is it for me that this man come to Troy?

ODYSSEUS

Only this bow of his will capture Troy.

NEOPTOLEMOS

So I won't be the one to sack the city, as you said?

ODYSSEUS

Not you without the bow, nor the bow without you.   115

NEOPTOLEMOS

Then it would have to become the object of our hunt, if this is so.[12]

ODYSSEUS

Yes, if you do this, you carry away two prizes for yourself.

NEOPTOLEMOS

What sort of prizes? If I knew, I would not refuse to act.

ODYSSEUS

You would be called both clever and noble at the same time.[13]

NEOPTOLEMOS

All right, let it go! I'll put aside all shame and do it.   120

ODYSSEUS

Do you remember, then, the advice I've given you?

NEOPTOLEMOS

Be sure I do, once I've agreed to it.

---

[12]   *"Then it would have to become the object of our hunt"*: Neoptolemos gives in to Odysseus in language that is unusually striking, because it includes the only occurrence in any Greek author of "become" instead of "be" in this kind of impersonal expression of necessity, as well as the only example in extant Sophoclean drama of "would have to" instead of "must" in such an expression. Neoptolemos seems reluctant to face squarely the consequences of what he admits is the reality of the situation ("if this is so"), as if the necessity to hunt the bow were not yet fully real and established in his mind.

[13]   The scholiast suggests that "clever" refers to the theft of the bow and "noble" to the sack of the city, or that for Odysseus "clever" refers generally to the power to deceive and deception is now something "noble." Certainly the word "clever" resonates with Odysseus' sophistic diction elsewhere in the Prologue (cf. on 14), and "both clever and noble" (119) is a characteristically Odyssean twist on the common, idiomatic phrase "both beautiful and noble," which typically approves aristocratic excellence.

ODYSSEUS

You remain here now and await that man;
I'll depart, so I'm not spotted in your company,
and I'll send the lookout back to the ship. If you seem to me   125
to be taking too much time, I'll send this same man
out again in the character of a merchant ship's captain,[14] so
he won't be recognized.
From him, my child,[15] as he speaks out craftily, receive   130
what is advantageous in his words, whenever he says something.
I'm going to the ship, now, and I'll leave these things to you.
May Hermes the Escort, the Trickster, guide the two of us,
and Victory Athena the City-Goddess, who always saves me.[16]

*(Exit Odysseus to the audience's left. The Chorus, fifteen sailors older than and
loyal to Neoptolemos, enter from the same side, singing.)[17]*

STROPHE A

CHORUS

A stranger in a strange land, what must I keep hidden,   135
master, and what must I say to a suspicious man?

---

14   *"a merchant ship's captain"*: a kind of unheroic figure often scorned in Greek
literature, because he is concerned with trade and profit (e.g. *Odyssey* 8.161-
64; cf. 111, above).

15   *"my child"*: Odysseus speaks persuasively, just as in 133 he uses the dual
form *nôin*, "the two of us" (cf. on 25), to assimilate Neoptolemos to his plot
and himself. Philoktetes calls Neoptolemos "my son" or "my child" 52
times in the play, and in effect wins a contest with Odysseus to see whose
"son" the "son of Achilles" really is.

16   Odysseus' anachronistic invocation of "Victory Athena the City-Goddess"
(*Nikê...Athana Polias*) would have reminded an Athenian audience of the
contemporary civic cults of "Athena the City-Goddess" (*Athêna Polias*) and
"Victory Athena" (*Athêna Nikê*). These cults were housed on the Athenian
acropolis in temples that were still under construction when the play was
produced in 409 BCE, and they were associated with fifth-century Athenian
imperialism and civic identity. Thus Odysseus, in his intrigue against
Philoktetes, is made, as it were, a representative not only of the Greek army
but of contemporary Athens. Cf. on 96-99.

17   The Chorus' entry song has an unusual structure in which their sung lyrics
alternate conversationally with Neoptolemos' chanted anapests. In 161,
however, the Chorus (or Chorus Leader) asks a question in anapests, and
in lines 201 and 210, the opening lines of strophê and antistrophê C, a sung
line is divided between the Chorus and Neoptolemos.

Show me.
For his craft surpasses other craft
and his thought other thought, the man who rules as king
with Zeus' divine scepter.   140
To you, child, all this ancient
power has come down; so tell me
how I must serve you.[18]

ANAPESTS

NEOPTOLEMOS
Now, if you perhaps wish to view the place
at the extreme end of the island, where he lies,   145
take courage and look; but when he arrives,
the dread traveler from these halls,
come forward whenever I signal with my hand,
and try to provide for the present moment.

ANTISTROPHE A

CHORUS
You mention my longtime concern, my king,   150
to keep watch for the moment that is especially critical for you.
But now
say what kind of dwelling he lives in
when he's at home, and where he is now.
It is not untimely that I learn this,   155
so he can't fall on me unexpectedly from somewhere.
What is his place, where does he stay? Does he
plant his footsteps at home or out of doors?

ANAPESTS

NEOPTOLEMOS
You see this home with doors at both ends,
his rocky bed-chamber.   160

CHORUS
Yes, but where is the poor man himself off to?

---

18   The Chorus call Neoptolemos "master" and "the man who rules as king,"
      but they also call him "child." They are older than he, perhaps veterans
      who once fought under the command of Achilles.

NEOPTOLEMOS

It is clear to me that he is dragging his
footsteps somewhere nearby, in need of food.
The story is that this is the nature
of the life he leads, painfully in his pain   165
hunting wild beasts with winged arrows,
and for him no
healer of evils draws near.

STROPHE B

CHORUS

For my part, I pity him, the way—
without any mortal to care for him   170
and unable to see the face of a comrade,
    wretched and always alone—
he is sick with a savage disease
and goes mad at every need
that arises. How, how does the ill-fated man hold out?   175
O devices of the gods,
O wretched races of mortals
for whom life exceeds due measure.

ANTISTROPHE B

This man, ranking, perhaps, behind   180
none of the leading households,
lies alone without a share of anything
good in life, apart from others,
with the shaggy or dappled
wild beasts, pitiable alike in both hunger   185
and pain and having heavy, incurable miseries.
And babbling Echo,
appearing far off, hears and responds
to his bitter cries of sorrow.[19]   190

ANAPESTS

NEOPTOLEMOS

None of this surprises me.
For those sufferings, if I have any understanding,

---

[19]   Echo's unselective responses can offer Philoktetes no human companionship
or consolation.

are divine and came to him
from savage-minded Chrysê[20];
as for his present, painful labors, with no one to care for him— 195
there's no way the gods are not concerned
lest this man draw against Troy too soon
the unopposable shafts of the gods,
until the time comes in which it is said
that the city must be conquered by them.[21] 200

STROPHE C

CHORUS
Quiet, child!

NEOPTOLEMOS
What's that?

CHORUS
Clearly it's a heavy sound, such as
might be comrade to an exhausted man
somewhere, here or there, in this place.
It hits me, it hits me—the unmistakable 205
voice of someone compelled to crawl on his way;
the heavy, far-off cry of a worn-out
man does not escape me. Yes, his lament rings out clearly.

ANTISTROPHE C

But, my child, think...

NEOPTOLEMOS
Of what? Tell me!

CHORUS
...something new. 210

---

[20] "*savage-minded Chrysê*": Chrysê is the nymph to whom the island of
Chrysê (cf. 270) near Lemnos was sacred. Philoktetes was bitten by the
serpent guarding her altar (cf. 194, 631-2, 1327-8). According to Pausanias,
Description of Greece 8.33.4, Chrysê had sunk beneath the sea by the time
he was writing in the second century C.E.

[21] "*...there's no way the gods are not concerned...that the city must be conquered
by them.*" Neoptolemos' conviction that the gods have caused Philoktetes'
suffering in order to delay the sack of Troy to "the time...in which it is
said / that the city must be conquered..." is clearly self-serving and without
any theological basis.

For the man is not far away from home but in this place;
he does not play music on a pipe
like a shepherd who walks the wild pastures,
but shouts out a far-sounding cry,   215
either stumbling and compelled in his anguish
or discerning the ship in its inhospitable
anchorage. His shout is something dreadful.

(Enter Philoktetes, not by one of the regular side passageways but from the mouth of his cave, represented by the skênê door)[22]

PHILOKTETES
Strangers!
Who in the world are you, who have put in with a sailor's oar   220
to this land that is uninhabited and without harbors?
What race or native land would I be right
to call yours? The style of your clothing is
Greek, most welcome and most dear to me,
but I wish to hear your voice. And don't shrink from me   225
or be frightened by my savage condition,
but take pity on a man wretched, alone,
deserted, so beset by troubles, without a companion or friend.
Speak, if you come as friends.
Answer me: it is not reasonable that I fail   230
in this, at least, from you or you from me.

NEOPTOLEMOS
Stranger, know this first, that we are
Greeks, since this is what you wish to learn.

PHILOKTETES.
O dearest sound! Oh, actually to be greeted
by such a man after so long a time!   235
What need, my child, brought you to put in
here? What impulse? What dearest of winds?
Tell me all this, so I may know who you are.

---

[22]   The cave's other opening is to be imagined as out of sight of the audience. Philoktetes' appearance—wildly unkempt, in rags, limping painfully and perhaps supporting his steps with the bow of Herakles or a crudely shaped branch—must have been visually striking to the audience as well as to Neoptolemos and the Chorus.

NEOPTOLEMOS

In race I am from Skyros,[23] surrounded
by the sea; I'm sailing home; and I call myself Neoptolemos,   240
the son of Achilles. Now you know it all.

PHILOKTETES.

Son of a most dear father, of a dear land,
foster-child of old Lykomedes,[24] on what
voyage have you put in to this land? Where are you sailing from?

NEOPTOLEMOS

Now, at any rate, I'm sailing from Troy.   245

PHILOKTETES.

What did you say? You certainly didn't sail
with us at the beginning of the campaign against Troy.

NEOPTOLEMOS

What, did you too take part in this toil?

PHILOKTETES

My child, don't you know me, don't you know whom you're looking
at?

NEOPTOLEMOS

No, how can I recognize a man I've never see   250

PHILOKTETES

So you've heard nothing, not even my name, not even the story
of my troubles, by which I've been utterly destroyed?

NEOPTOLEMOS

Understand that I know nothing of what you're asking me.

PHILOKTETES.

Oh, I am truly wretched and hateful to the gods!
Not even a rumor of my situation got through   255
to my home or to anywhere in the land of Greece.
But those who impiously abandoned me

---

23   *Skyros*: an island about 35 miles east of Euboia and 75 miles SSW of
      Lemnos.
24   *Lykomedes*: king of Skyros and father of Neoptolemos' mother,
      Deidamia.

keep silent and laugh at me,[25] while my disease
always blossoms and increases in strength.[26]
My child, son whose father was Achilles,   260
here I am before you, that man whom perhaps you hear of
as master of the arms of Herakles—
Philoktetes, the son of Poias, whom the
two generals and the Kephallenian king[27]
shamelessly cast out into this isolation, wasting away   265
with a savage disease, struck by the savage
mark of the man-destroying serpent.
Those men, my son, went off and left me here
alone with this disease, when they put in to this place
with their naval fleet from sea-washed Chrysê.   270
Gladly, then, when they saw me sleeping on the shore
in a sheltering cave, after a rough voyage,
they went off and left me behind, once they had set out
the sort of things you would offer a wretched man— a few rags
and a small helping of food, too. May such things happen
      to them!   275
What sort of awakening, my child, do you think
I then awoke to from my sleep, when they had gone away?
What tears do you think I burst into, what laments for my troubles,
when I saw the ships I'd sailed in command of
all gone, and not a man in the place, no one   280
to assist me, no one who could help me in my suffering
to support my disease. Looking everywhere
I found nothing at hand except anguish,
but of this a great abundance, my child.
Now time went on and on for me, and   285
I had to tend to my own needs alone, under
this poor roof. This bow found what I

---

[25] *"impiously abandoned me"*: Philoktetes' claim is in striking contrast to that
of Odysseus in 8-11. *"laugh at me"*: to be laughed at or mocked by one's
enemies is especially humiliating. Cf. 1023, 1125; Sophokles, *Ajax* 79, 303,
367, *Antigone* 483, 647; Euripides, *Medea* 383, 404, 798, 1241, 1355, 1363.

[26] *"my disease always blossoms"*: Philoktetes has an idiosyncratic way of speaking
of his disease as an independent, living entity, capable of agency and
separate from himself. Cf. 313, 743-4, 758-9.

[27] *"the Kephallenian king"*: Odysseus, whose kingdom included the island of
Kephallênia, close to Ithaca.

needed for my belly, shooting down
winged doves; in addition, whatever an arrow
from my bowstring might hit, I would crawl to   290
myself in my misery, dragging my wretched
foot. And if I had to get something to drink
or break up wood, when frost was spread on the ground,
as in winter, I would crawl out in my misery and
manage this. Then there would be no fire on hand,   295
but rubbing one stone hard against another, with difficulty
I made the invisible light appear, which is what always saves me.[28]
To dwell with a roof over my head and a fire
provides everything, except that I not be diseased.
Come, my child, now learn about the island, too.   300
No sailor puts in to this place willingly;
there's no anchorage at all, no place to sail where
he will sell for a profit or receive hospitality.
Sensible men do not make voyages here.
Now perhaps someone puts in against his will: many things   305
like this could happen in a long, human lifetime.
These men, whenever they come, my child, pity me
in words, and in their pity they hand over
a small portion of food or some clothing;
but when I mention it, no one is willing to do this—   310
to save me and bring me home; but this is the tenth year now
in which I perish in my misery from the evils
of hunger, while feeding my insatiable disease.
This is what the sons of Atreus and violent Odysseus
have done to me, my son[29]; may the Olympian gods some day   315

---

[28] *"…which is what always saves me."* Philoktetes describes fire in the same
words Odysseus uses at 134 of *"Victory Athena the City-Goddess, who always
saves me."*

[29] *"violent Odysseus"*: literally, "the violence (*bia*) of Odysseus." This
traditional kind of naming periphrasis, derived from Homeric epic (where
it is ethically neutral), seems to characterize Odysseus negatively both for
abandoning Philoktetes on Lemnos in the first place and for plotting to take
him to Troy against his will. The same phrase ("the violence of Odysseus")
occurs at 321 and 592, and there is a similar expression, "bring by violence,"
at 563, 945, and 985; cf. 90, 92, and 103.

grant that they suffer such things in payment for my suffering.[30]

CHORUS
I think that I too pity you just like the strangers
who have come previously, child of Poias.

NEOPTOLEMOS
I myself am a witness to these words,
I know they are true, since I have found the sons   320
of Atreus and violent Odysseus to be evil men.

PHILOKTETES
What, do you too have some claim against the accursed
sons of Atreus? Are you angry at what you have suffered?

NEOPTOLEMOS
May I one day satisfy my anger with my hand,
so that Mykênai and Sparta may know that   325
Skyros too is the mother of mighty men.[31]

PHILOKTETES
Well said, my child! But why have you come
to accuse them in such great anger?

NEOPTOLEMOS
Son of Poias, I will tell you all, though it is hard for me to tell,
how I was openly insulted by them when I came.   330
For when Fate determined that Achilles die—

PHILOKTETES
Oh! Say no more, until I learn
this first: is the offspring of Peleus dead?

NEOPTOLEMOS
He is dead, at the hands of no man, but of a god,
Shot by an arrow, as they say, overcome by Phoibos.[32]   335

---

30   Philoktetes closes his speech as he began, with a reference to the gods. His wish in 315-6 seems to imply that despite his suffering, he considers them to be morally relevant and just.

31   *Mykênai* is the home of Agamemnon, *Sparta* of Menelaos, and *Skyros* of Neoptolemos.

32   *Phoibos*: "pure" or "bright," an old epithet of Apollo that came to be used as an alternative proper name. In the usual version of the story, Paris shot the arrow, which was guided to its target by Apollo. Cf. *Iliad* 22.359-60.

PHILOKTETES
Both he who killed and he who died are noble.
But I am at a loss, my child, whether I should first
lament for that man or ask about your suffering.

NEOPTOLEMOS
You poor man, I think your own sorrows are enough
for you not to groan for those of your friends.   340

PHILOKTETES
You're right. So tell me again about the matter
in which they insolently wronged and insulted you.

NEOPTOLEMOS
They came for me in a ship whose prow was decked with garlands,
brilliant Odysseus and the man who reared my father,[33]
saying—whether truly or, after all, an empty falsehood—   345
that it would not be right, since my father had perished,
for any one but me to take the towers of Troy.
When they said these things in this way, stranger, they stopped
me for no long time from setting sail quickly—
especially because of my longing to see the dead man   350
still unburied; for I'd never set eyes on him;
then too, in addition, what they said was attractive,
that if I went, I would take the towers of Troy.
It was already the second day of my voyage,
and I was putting in with my wind-driven oar   355
to cruel Sigeion[34]; at once the whole army surrounded
me and greeted me as I landed, swearing they saw
the dead Achilles alive once again.
Now he lay there dead, but I, the ill-fated one,
when I had wept for him, went to the sons   360
of Atreus without delay, in friendship, as was reasonable,
and asked for my father's arms and the rest of his possessions.
But they, alas, spoke most audaciously:
"Seed of Achilles, the rest of your father's things
are yours to take, but another man is now master   365

---

[33] *"the man who reared my father"*: Phoinix. See *Iliad* 9.485-95.

[34] *"cruel Sigeion"*: a promontory west of Troy, about 125 miles (a two-day sail) from Skyros. It is *"cruel"* either because it was the site of Achilles' tomb or in anticipation of what Neoptolemos says happened to him after he landed.

of those weapons, the offspring of Laertes.[35]
And I, bursting into tears, rise at once
in heavy anger, and feeling great pain I say,
"You miserable man, did you dare to give my weapons
to someone else instead of me, without asking me?"   370
And Odysseus (for he happened to be nearby) said,
"Yes, boy, these men gave them to me, justly;
for I was there and saved them—and him too."
I was angry and at once began to hurl insults
at all of them, leaving out nothing,   375
if that man were going to rob me of my arms.
Stung by what he heard, though not quick to anger,
he was brought to that point and answered in this way:
"You were not where we were, but off where you shouldn't have
      been;
and as for these arms, since you speak with so bold a mouth, 380
you will never sail back with them to Skyros."
After hearing myself insulted with such evils,
I'm sailing home, robbed of what was mine
by the vilest offspring of vile ancestors, Odysseus.[36]
And I don't blame him as much as those in office: 385
a city as a whole belongs to its leaders,
as does an entire army; and those mortals who are
disorderly, become evil through the words of their teachers.[37]

---

[35] *"offspring of Laertes"*: Odysseus. Here as elsewhere it is difficult, if not
impossible, to know whether, or to what extent, Neoptolemos is telling
the "truth" in his lying tale, or even whether there is any "truth" to tell.
In the usual version of the myth, which is the background of Sophokles'
Ajax, Odysseus was awarded the arms of Achilles for his services to the
Greek army and the harm he caused the Trojans. In *Philoktetes*, however,
would Neoptolemos be helping the Greeks and obeying Odysseus, if this
were the case? Yet later in the play, when Philoktetes asks Neoptolemos
if he really will be the ally of the men who "violated you outrageously, /
stripping you of your father's special honor" (1364-65), Neoptolemos does
not correct or contradict him.

[36] Philoktetes refers to the story that Odysseus really was the son of the cunning
Sisyphos, who in *Odyssey* 11. 593-600 is among the arch-transgressors being
punished in Hades, rather than of Laertes, who was said to have bought
him from Sisyphos (417; cf. 624-5, 1311).

[37] Some scholars have argued that 385-88 are not by Sophokles but were
interpolated into the text sometime in antiquity, on the grounds that they

I've said what I have to say; may the man who hates the sons
of Atreus be as much a friend to the gods as he is to me.   390

STROPHE

CHORUS

All-nourishing mountain goddess Earth,
mother of Zeus himself,
you who rule the great Pactôlos rich in gold,[38]
there too, lady mother, I called on you,   395
when the insolent outrage of the sons of Atreus
was moving with all its force against this man,
when they were treacherously giving away his ancestral armor—
blessed goddess, you who ride
on bull-slaying lions—to the son of Laertes,   400
an object of the highest reverence.[39]

PHILOKTETES

It seems you have sailed here, strangers, with

---

seem intrusive and appear to exculpate Odysseus as merely following his
commanders' orders, a sentiment out of keeping with the way Neoptolemos
and Philoktetes speak of Odysseus elsewhere in the play. On the other hand,
Neoptolemos may (consciously or unconsciously) be evading responsibility
for his own obedience to the orders of *his* commander, Odysseus, even
though this would mean that he includes himself among "those mortals
who are disorderly." The reference to a "city" and the use of the Attic
idiom, "those in office" (385), would have reminded Sophokles' audience
of their own city, as would other passages in the play (see on 96-99, 134,
1328).

[38] *"the great Pactôlos"* : a river in Lydia, in Asia Minor, from which gold dust
was extracted.

[39] In this strophê the Chorus invoke a goddess who combines features of
Earth, the "great mother" of the gods, and Cybele, a Phrygian goddess
identified with the Greek Rhea, mother of Zeus. Cybele was worshipped in
Asia Minor, especially in Sardis, which was situated on the east bank of the
Pactôlos. In their claim to have called on her near Troy, when Neoptolemos
was being robbed of his arms by the sons of Atreus, the Chorus support
their master's lying story with what almost amounts to a false oath. This is
highly unusual and paralleled in extant Sophoclean tragedy only at *Electra*
47, where Orestes tells the Paidagogos to "add an oath" in support of his
false report of Orestes' death in the Pythian Games; and at *The Women of
Trachis* 399, where Lichas, even though he is lying, calls on "great Zeus"
to "know" that he is truly telling Deianeira all that he knows about Herakles
and Iole.

a token of grief that clearly matches my own,[40]
and you are in harmony with me, so I can recognize   405
these as actions of the sons of Atreus and of Odysseus.
For I know well that he would apply his tongue
to every evil speech and every villainy by which
he might achieve an end that is in no way just.[41]
No, this doesn't surprise me at all, but I wonder   410
how Ajax, if he was there to see it, put up with this.[42]

NEOPTOLEMOS
Stranger, he was no longer living; I would never
have been stripped of these arms, while that man was alive.

PHILOKTETES
What did you say? Is he too dead and gone?

NEOPTOLEMOS
Think of him as no longer seeing the light of life.   415

PHILOKTETES
Alas for wretched me. But no, not the offspring of Tydeus,[43]
or the son of Sisyphos who was bought by Laertes[44]—
they will never die, for these men ought not to be living in the first
   place.

---

[40]   "*a token*": one of two parts into which an object had been broken, which
could be fitted together with the other part as a proof of identity or a sign
of guest-friendship.

[41]   See on 99.

[42]   The reference is to Ajax, son of Telamon, the greater Ajax (in contrast to
Ajax, son of Oileus, the lesser Ajax), who in the usual version of the myth,
as told in Sophokles' *Ajax*, committed suicide when the arms of Achilles
were awarded to Odysseus. See on 365-66.

[43]   "*the offspring of Tydeus*" : Diomedes, a frequent companion of Odysseus in
duplicitous actions, such as the night-spying adventure in Book 10 of the
Iliad and the theft from Troy, narrated in the *Little Iliad* (see below, p. 89,
n. 2) of the Palladion, a small statue of Athena, the possession of which by
the Trojans protected their city. In Euripides' *Philoktetes*, he accompanied
Odysseus to Lemnos to fetch Philoktetes. In 591-4, the "Merchant"
reports that Odysseus and Diomedes have set sail, after swearing to bring
Philoktetes to Troy by persuasion or force.

[44]   The scholiast on 417 says that Antikleia was pregnant by Sisyphos when
Laertes married her, "having given many gifts." (See on 384).

NEOPTOLEMOS

Certainly not, be sure of it! But in fact they now
are flourishing greatly in the Argive army.   420

PHILOKTETES

Alas! But what of my good old friend,
Nestor the Pylian,[45] is he alive? For this man might perhaps
have prevented their evils by his wise counsels.

NEOPTOLEMOS

Yes, he's alive, but he's badly off now, since his Antilochos
is dead and gone, who was his offspring.   425

PHILOKTETES

Oh, you've mentioned the two men just now whom
I would least have wished to hear were dead.[46]
Alas, alas! What must we look for, when these men
are dead but Odysseus lives, who ought
to be dead himself instead of them.   430

NEOPTOLEMOS

That man is a cunning wrestler, but cunning plans,
Philoktetes, are often tripped up and thwarted.

PHILOKTETES

Come, tell me, by the gods, where was Patroklos in all this,
in your time of need, who was dearest of all to your father?

NEOPTOLEMOS

He too was dead. In a brief word   435
I'll tell you this: war takes no wicked man
willingly, but always the good and useful ones.

PHILOKTETES

I bear you witness and, for just this reason,
I'll ask about a man who is worthless
but terribly clever with his tongue—how he is doing now.   440

---

[45] "*Nestor the Pylian*": Nestor, King of Pylos. In the *Iliad* his son Antilochos (see 424) is a leading Greek warrior and close friend of Achilles. Antilochos' death at the hands of the Trojan ally Memnon, Memnon's subsequent death at the hands of Achilles, and Achilles' death at the hands of Paris and Apollo (cf. *Iliad* 22.359-60) were narrated in the *Aithiopis*, the epic following the *Iliad* and preceding the *Little Iliad* in the "Epic Cycle." See below, Interpretive Essay, p. 89, n. 2.

[46] "*the two men*": Ajax and Antilochos

NEOPTOLEMOS

Of whom else do you speak, except Odysseus?

PHILOKTETES

I didn't mean him, but there was a certain Thersites
who would never choose to speak briefly, even when
no one wanted him to speak at all.[47] Do you know if he happens to
  be alive?

NEOPTOLEMOS

I didn't see him myself, but I heard that he's still living.   445

PHILOKTETES

He would be! Nothing evil has ever perished,
but the gods protect them carefully and well;
somehow they enjoy turning back from Hades
that which is cunning and villainous, but they always
send send away what is useful and just.   450
How should I understand these things, how praise them, when
praising the actions of the gods I find the gods evil?

NEOPTOLEMOS

For my part, son of an Oitaian father,[48]
I'll be on my guard from now on and view
Ilion and the sons of Atreus from far away.   455
Where the worse man is stronger than the noble,
and what is good perishes and the coward is master—
I'll never embrace or make friends of these men!
From now on rocky Skyros will be enough
for me, and I'll be happily at home there.   460
Now I'm off to my ship, and to you, child of Poias,

---

47   "*Thersites*": "the ugliest man who came beneath Ilion; / he was bow-legged,
     lame in one foot, and his two shoulders / were curved, hunched together
     over his chest; his head / above was pointed and had a sparse growth of
     hair. / He was especially hated by Achilles and Odysseus," because of
     his habit of speaking "out of turn, in a disorderly fashion, and quarreling
     with the kings" (*Iliad* 2.213-4, 216-20). In the *Aithiopis* and other sources,
     Achilles kills Thersites. Here again, as in the story of the arms of Achilles,
     Sophokles plays against the traditional story and leaves it unclear whether,
     or to what extent, Neoptolemos is telling the truth.

48   "*Oitaian father*": Mt. Oita, the site of Herakles' pyre and apotheosis (727-9),
     was located in Poias' kingdom of Malis.

farewell, a hearty farewell; and may the gods
free you from your disease, as you yourself desire.

(to the Chorus)

Let's be going, so that we may set forth
whenever a god allows us a good sailing   465

PHILOKTETES
Are you going already, my child?

NEOPTOLEMOS
                                                    Yes, now is the opportune moment
to watch for the chance to sail from close by the ship, not at a dis-
tance.

PHILOKTETES
By your father, by your mother, my child,
and by anything at home that is dear to you,
I beseech you as a suppliant,[49] don't leave me alone in this way,   470
isolated among these evils that you see
and all the others you've heard I live with.
Make me at least your secondary concern. The unpleasantness,
I know, is great, if you take me along in this way,
but all the same bring yourself to do it. Those who are noble   475
hate what is shameful and win glory by their generosity.
If you fail to do this, the reproach for you will be ugly,
but if you do it, my son, you will gain the greatest glory
as a reward, if I reach the land of Oita alive.
Come, it will not be a full day's burden for you;   480
bring yourself to do it. Take me and throw me wherever you
    wish,
into the bilge, the prow, the stern, wherever I
will cause the least pain for those who are with me.
Nod your consent, my child; by Zeus himself, the god of
    suppliants,
be persuaded. I'm on my knees before you, even though I'm   485

---

[49]   Philoktetes probably stoops to embrace Neoptolemos' knees with one hand
        while reaching toward his chin with the other, in the traditional posture of a
        suppliant placing himself in the power and under the protection of another.
        He may, however, remain standing until 485, when he says explicitly, "I
        am on my knees before you." Or perhaps he first stoops at 470, rises a few
        lines later, and then falls to his knees again at 485.

powerless and wretchedly lame. No, don't leave me alone
in such isolation, apart from the tread of human beings,
but save me by bringing me either to your home
or to Chalkôdôn's Euboian dwelling.[50]
From there it will be a short voyage to Oita   490
and the ridge of Trachis and the fair-flowing
Spercheios, where you may show me to my dear father.[51]
For a long time now I've feared that he
may be gone from me. I summoned him repeatedly   495
by those who came here, sending a suppliant's prayers
that he sail here himself to save me and bring me home.
But either he's dead or, as I think likely, the messengers
considered my plight unimportant and hurried to their own
   homes.
Now I come to you as my messenger and at the same time
   my escort: 500
you be the one to save me, you take pity on me, seeing
that all things are full of fear for mortals, and of the danger
that just as they fare well, so they may suffer the reverse.
A man should look for terrible troubles when he is free from
   suffering;
and whenever someone is living well, that is when he should   505
be most on guard not to be destroyed unawares.

ANTISTROPHE[52]

CHORUS
Have pity, my king; he has spoken
of a struggle with many pitiful
toils; may none of my friends encounter such things.
If, my king, you hate the cruel sons of Atreus,   510

---

[50]   "Chalkôdôn": a King of Euboia in Poias' generation. Cf. *Iliad* 2.541,
4.464.

[51]   "*Trachis*": a region between Mt. Oita and the Malian gulf through which
the *Spercheios* river flows after skirting the Oitaian heights, which are called
by Herodotos (7.198) the "Trachinian Cliffs." It is the setting of Sophokles'
The Women of Trachis.

[52]   507-18 correspond metrically to lines 391-402. Just as in those lines
the Chorus assist in Neoptolemos' effort to gain Philoktetes' trust, so
here, though the pity they express may be genuine, they mean to help
Neoptolemos bring Philoktetes to Troy.

I, for my part, turning
their evil action
to this man's great profit,
would transport him home   515
where he longs to go,
on a well-equipped, swift ship, escaping
the righteous anger of the gods.

NEOPTOLEMOS

Beware. Now you are easy about it,
but when you are filled with the presence of the disease,   520
you may then no longer appear the same as in these words.

CHORUS

No, not at all. There's no way you'll ever be able
to reproach me justly with this reproach.

NEOPTOLEMOS

Well, I would be ashamed to appear to the stranger
less ready than you to serve his critical need.   525
If it seems best, let him set forth swiftly and let us set sail;
the ship will bring him and will not refuse.
May the gods only bring us safely out of
this land to wherever we might wish to sail.

PHILOKTETES

You friendliest of days and sweetest of men,   530
you sailor friends, I wish I could make clear to you
by some action how friendly you have made me toward you.[53]
Let's go, my son, once the two of us have done reverence
to my dwelling that is no dwelling inside the cave,[54] so you may
   learn
how I managed to stay alive and with what courage I was born.   535
I don't think that another man than myself, if he merely
had set eyes on this sight, could have endured these things,
but I have slowly learned by necessity to embrace my troubles.

---

[53]   *"you sailor friends…"*: Philoktetes previously called Neoptolemos and his
       men "strangers" (*xenoi*), but now he speaks of them as 'friends" (*philoi*)
       and of himself as reciprocating their friendship.

[54]   *"once the two of us have done reverence"*: Philoktetes uses the dual form, thus
       placing Neoptolemos and himself on an equal basis and, in effect, competing
       with Odysseus' duals at 25 and 133. See the notes on 25 and 1436-7.

CHORUS
  Hold on, you two, let's wait; two men
  are coming, one a sailor from your ship   540
  and the other a foreigner; after you've heard them, then go in.

(Enter the "Merchant" from the audience's left, accompanied by a sailor)

MERCHANT
  Son of Achilles, I told my fellow traveler, here,
  who was guarding your ship with two others,
  to show me where you might be,
  since I encountered you unexpectedly,   545
  when by chance I anchored off the same coast.
  I'm sailing as a merchant captain, with a small ship's company,
  from Ilion to my home in Peparêthos,
  rich in grapes[55]; when I heard from the sailors that
  they all were members of your crew, I thought it best   550
  not to continue my voyage in silence, before
  speaking with you and receiving a fair recompense.
  You doubtless know nothing of what concerns you,
  what new plans the Argives have for you—
  and not only plans but actions already being   555
  implemented and no longer delayed.

NEOPTOLEMOS
  Stranger, the kindness of your forethought will remain
  in my grateful memory, if I am not ignoble by nature;
  but tell me about the actions you mentioned, so I may learn
  what startling new plan of the Argives you can tell me of.   560

MERCHANT
  They've gone after you in a well-equipped ship,
  the old man Phoinix and the sons of Theseus.[56]

NEOPTOLEMOS
  To bring me back by force or with words?

---

55 *Peparêthos*: a small island about 20 miles NE of Euboia and 40 miles NW
    of Skyros, famous for its wine.

56 *"the sons of Theseus"*: Demophon, King of Athens, and his brother Akamas.
    They might be considered hostile to Neoptolemos, because in one version
    of the myth their father, Theseus, was killed in Skyros by Lykomedes,
    Neoptolemos' maternal grandfather.

MERCHANT
I don't know, but I'm here to report what I heard.

NEOPTOLEMOS
Are Phoinix and those who sail with him so eager   565
to please the sons of Atreus by doing this?

MERCHANT
Know that this is happening now, not coming in the future.

NEOPTOLEMOS
How, then, was Odysseus not ready to sail for this purpose
as his own messenger? Did some fear hold him back?

MERCHANT
No, when I put out to sea, that man and the son   570
of Tydeus were setting forth after another man.[57]

NEOPTOLEMOS
Who, then, was this man against whom Odysseus himself was sailing?

MERCHANT
There was a certain—but first tell me who this man
is, and whatever you say, don't speak loudly.

NEOPTOLEMOS
Stranger, this man here before you is the famous Philoktetes!   575

MERCHANT
Ask me nothing more, but sail away as quickly
as possible and get yourself out of this land.

PHILOKTETES
What is he saying, my son? What business does the sailor
carry on with you secretly in whispers?

NEOPTOLEMOS
I don't know yet what he is saying, but he must say   580
what he has to say openly, to you and me and these men here.

MERCHANT
Seed of Achilles, don't accuse me to the army
for saying what I shouldn't have said. I do many useful things
for them and receive many benefits in return, as a poor man would.

---

[57]   *"the son / of Tydeus"*: see on 416.

NEOPTOLEMOS

I'm their enemy, and this man is my great   585
friend, because he hates the sons of Atreus.[58]
If you've come to me with good intentions, you must
hide from us nothing that you've heard.

MERCHANT

See what you're doing, my son.

NEOPTOLEMOS

                          I've been considering it for a
long time now.

MERCHANT

I make you responsible for this.

NEOPTOLEMOS

                         Do so, but speak.   590

MERCHANT

I am speaking. It's against this man that those two you hear about
are sailing, the son of Tydeus and violent Odysseus—
sworn to take him back either by persuasion
of speech or by powerful constraint of force.
All the Achaians heard Odysseus saying   595
this clearly, for he was more confident
than the other that he would accomplish this.

NEOPTOLEMOS

But why were the sons of Atreus
so intent on this man after so long a time,
a man whom long ago they already had thrown away?   600
What longing came over them? Was it the gods' violence
and righteous anger, which punish evil deeds?

MERCHANT

I will instruct you, for perhaps you have not
heard all this. There was a seer of noble birth,
a son of Priam, Helenos by name;   605
Odysseus, who hears all shameful and disgraceful

---

[58]   *"this man is...the sons of Atreus"*: cf. 389-90; here, for the first time,
Neoptolemos speaks of Philoktetes as a "friend" (*philos*), rather than a
"stranger" (*xenos*), as in 412. See on 531-2.

words spoken about him, went out alone in the night, took him
by treachery, and brought him bound to show off
publicly to the Argives, a fine prey.
Helenos then prophesied to them all the other things   610
and especially that they would never sack the towers of Troy,
unless they should persuade this man by speech and bring
him from this island where he now dwells.[59]
When the son of Laertes heard that the seer
had said these things, he quickly promised   615
to fetch this man and show him to the Achaians—
probably, he thought, taking him as a willing prisoner,
but if he should refuse, against his will; and if he failed in this,
he would allow whoever wanted to cut off his head.[60]
You've heard the whole story, my son; I advise you to hurry   620
for your own sake and that of anyone you care about.

PHILOKTETES

Alas for wretched me! Did that man, that utter plague,
swear to convey me to the Achaians by persuasion?
No, at this rate, I'll be persuaded to come back up into the light
from Hades when I have died, just like his father.[61]   625

MERCHANT

I don't know about this, but I'll be off to my ship,
and may a god assist you both as best he can.

(Exit the "Merchant" and his companion to the audience's left)

---

59   In the Prologue, Odysseus suggested only that the bow and Neoptolemos
were needed to sack Troy. Now the "Merchant" says explicitly that
Philoktetes and the bow are required; Neoptolemos gives a different
version of this prophecy in 1329-41. It is impossible to be certain what
Helenos actually said, because both the "Merchant" and Neoptolemos
speak persuasively and shape the prophecy to their own purposes.

60   "*to cut off his head*": in Homer Odysseus twice makes a similar offer, at *Il.*
2.259, if he should not punish Thersites, and at *Od.* 16.102, if he should fail
to take vengeance on the Suitors.

61   "*his father*": as the scholiast on 625 tells the story, when Sisyphos was about
to die, he told his wife to leave him unburied; then, when he went down
to the underworld, he accused her of not having done what was customary
and asked Aidoneus (Hades) for permission to go back and punish her.
When allowed to do so, he stayed there until he went down again "by
necessity."

PHILOKTETES
Is this not strange, my child, that the son of Laertes
ever expected to bring me in his ship with soft words
and show me off in the midst of the Argives?   630
No! I would sooner listen to what I hate the most,
the serpent that crippled me in this way.
But that man would say and dare anything,
and now I know that he will come here.
My child, let us depart, so that a great sea   635
may separate us from the ship of Odysseus.
Let's go; timely haste, once toil
has ceased, brings tranquillity and sleep.

NEOPTOLEMOS
Then whenever the headwind lets up,
we'll set forth, but now it's against us.   640

PHILOKTETES
It's always good sailing, when you flee from troubles.

NEOPTOLEMOS
I know, but the wind is against them, too.

PHILOKTETES
No wind is against pirates, when they
can ravage and plunder violently.

NEOPTOLEMOS
Well, if it seems best, let's go, once you've taken from within   645
whatever you especially need and desire.

PHILOKTETES
Yes, I need some things, even if there's not much to choose from.

NEOPTOLEMOS
What is there that is not on board my ship?

PHILOKTETES
I have a certain herb with which I always
calm this wound of mine and soothe it entirely.   650

NEOPTOLEMOS
Well, bring it out. What else do you desire to take?

PHILOKTETES
Any arrow that may have slipped away and been

forgotten, so I don't leave it for anyone else to take.

NEOPTOLEMOS
Is this the famous bow that you now are holding?

PHILOKTETES
Yes, this is it; there's no other but what I carry in my two hands.   655

NEOPTOLEMOS
Is it possible for me to see it from up close
and handle it and show it reverence like a god?

PHILOKTETES
Yes, this shall be granted to you, my child,
and anything else in my power that may be good for you.

NEOPTOLEMOS
I truly desire it, but I desire it in this way: 660
if it is right, I would want to; if not, let it go.

PHILOKTETES
You speak with reverence, my child, and it *is* right for you,
who alone have granted me to see this light
of the sun and live, to see the land of Oita,
my old father, my friends; who raised me above   665
my enemies when I was beneath their feet.
Take courage, you will be able to touch this bow
and give it to the one who gave it to you, and to boast
that you alone of mortals handled it because of your nobility.
For I myself gained possession of it by doing a good deed.[62]   670

NEOPTOLEMOS
I am not burdened by having seen you and taken you as a friend:
whoever knows how to return a benefit he has received,
would be a friend better than any possession.[63]
Go inside, if you wish.

---

[62] As a youth Philoktetes kindled the pyre of Herakles on Mt. Oita, in return
for which he received Herakles' bow and arrows. Cf. 801-803.

[63] "*I am not burdened...better than any possession*": these lines contain a
complex pun on the name Philoktetes, which is composed of the elements
philo-, "(own, dear) friend" and *ktêma / ktaomai* ("possession" / "gain
possession"). When Neoptolemos says that he has "taken [Philoktetes]
as a friend" and especially that "whoever knows how to return a benefit
he has received / would be a friend better than any possession," he both
echoes Philoktetes' statement that he "gained possession of" the bow "by

PHILOKTETES

                Yes, and I shall lead you in, too;
my disease longs to have you standing beside me.   675

(Neoptolemos and Philoktetes enter the cave together)

                             STROPHE A

CHORUS

I have heard in story, but certainly never seen
the man who once approached the god's own marriage bed—
heard how the all-conquering son of Kronos
took and bound him
on a deadly, whirling wheel[64];
but I know of no other mortal, of whom I have heard or seen,   680
who has met with a fate more hateful than this man's:
he did nothing to anyone, no robbery,
but being a just man among just men,
perished undeservedly in this way.   685
I'm amazed at how,

---

doing a good deed," and puns on the name of Philoktetes as meaning, "(gaining) possession of a friend." At the same time, however, the name Philoktetes might also mean "a friend who possesses," calling to mind his having possession of the bow and suggesting that Neoptolemos' taking Philoktetes as a friend is related to this possession. Furthermore, Neoptolemos' use of the word "possession" in 673 recalls Odysseus' use of the same word in 81, when he tells Neoptolemos that "the possession of victory is sweet to gain," while urging him to "be the thief of the invincible weapons" (78). At this point in the play, Neoptolemos' friendship for Philoktetes is part of his opportunistic ruse to gain possession of the bow and its owner. Later, however, after Philoktetes offers and Neoptolemos accepts the bow in a ritual gesture that formally establishes their friendship (776), and Neoptolemos pities Philoktetes' suffering and helplessness during his paroxysm (806), Neoptolemos' friendship becomes genuine and eventually is the basis of his relationship with Philoktetes for the rest of the play. In ordinary Greek terms, such a friendship consists mainly of reciprocal obligations to help and support one another and to have the same friends and enemies.

64   The Chorus allusively cite Ixion as a case of suffering parallel to Philoktetes, but actually he is a counter-example, a paradigm of ingratitude, since he repaid Zeus' kindness in purifying him for the murder of his father-in-law, Deioneus, by trying to rape Hera. He was unsuccessful in the attempt, and Zeus had him bound by Hermes on a wheel of fire in the land of the dead.

how in the world, listening in solitude
to the waves beating around him,
how he kept his hold on a life
so full of tears;   690

where he was all alone and had no one walking nearby,
no one in the land as a neighbor to his troubles,
beside whom he could bewail the disease
with groans that called forth a response--
the disease that gnawed into him and drained his blood--   695
no one who could put to sleep, with gentle herbs
taken from the nurturing earth,
the burning flow of blood oozing from the ulcer
of his wild beast of a foot,
if some paroxysm should befall him.   700
He would creep this way and that,
sometimes crawling
like a child without his dear nurse
to a place where there might be something to ease
his need, when the spirit-devouring   705
plague abated,

not gathering for food a crop sown in the holy earth
or other things that we men provide for ourselves by toil,
except if he sometimes could get food for his belly   710
with winged arrows from his swift-shooting bow.
O wretched life,
he did not enjoy a drink of poured wine for ten whole years,   715
but looking around to find a stagnant pool of water,
each time he would make his way to it.

Now he has met with the son of noble men,
and after those sufferings will end up great and happy;   720
that man, in the fullness of many months, is bringing him
in a sea-crossing ship to his native land,
the haunt of the Malian nymphs,   725
and to the banks of the Spercheios, where the man with the
  bronze shield

drew near to the gods as a god blazing with divine fire,
above the heights of Oita.[65]

(Neoptolemos and Philoktetes re-enter from the cave)

NEOPTOLEMOS
Come, if you wish. Why are you silent in this way   730
for no reason, why do you stand dumbstruck?

PHILOKTETES
Ah, ah, ah, ah!

NEOPTOLEMOS
What is it?

PHILOKTETES
          Nothing terrible. Go on, my child.

NEOPTOLEMOS
You're not in pain, are you, because your disease is with you?

PHILOKTETES
No, I'm not; just now I think I'm feeling better.   735
O gods!

NEOPTOLEMOS
          Why do you groan in this way and call on the gods?[66]

PHILOKTETES
To come as saviors and be gentle to us.
Ah, ah, ah, ah!

NEOPTOLEMOS
What is happening to you? Will you be silent in this way   740
and not speak? You appear to be having some bad trouble.

PHILOKTETES
I'm lost, my child, and I won't be able to hide
the trouble from you. Aah! It goes through me,
it goes through me! O wretched me!

---

65   *"banks of the Spercheios"*: see on 492. In 727-9 the Chorus allude to the
     apotheosis of Herakles, after Philoktetes had kindled his pyre (cf. 801-803).
     This allusion, at the mid-point of the play, looks forward to the epiphany
     of the god Herakles in the final scene.

66   On *antilabê* in 732, 736, and elsewhere in this scene, see on 54.

I'm lost, child! My child, I'm being eaten alive! Aah! 745
Aah, aah, aah, aah, aah!![67]
By the gods, my child, if you have some sword
handy, strike at the end of my foot and
cut it off as quickly as possible; don't spare my life!
Come, my son! 750

NEOPTOLEMOS
What is this new thing that comes so suddenly and makes
you cry out in this way and groan for yourself?

PHILOKTETES
You know, my child!

NEOPTOLEMOS
    What is it?

PHILOKTETES
        You know, my child!

NEOPTOLEMOS
           What's wrong with you?
I don't know.

PHILOKTETES
    How could you not know? Aah, aah, aah![68]

NEOPTOLEMOS
The burden of your sickness is terrible! 755

PHILOKTETES
Yes, it is terrible and unspeakable. But take pity on me.

NEOPTOLEMOS
What should I do, then?

PHILOKTETES
      Don't abandon me, out of fear!
She comes after an interval, the disease, perhaps when she's

---

[67] "*Aah, aah, aah, aah, aah!*": a remarkable line in Greek, consisting of one
long, grammatically unarticulated, but metrically correct cry of agony, the
sounds of which (*apappapai papa papa papa papai*) suggest words meaning
"daddy" (*papa*) and "child" (*pais*).

[68] The triple change of speaker in 753 and quadruple occurrence of the word
"know" in 753-54 suggest both the special intensity of Philoktetes' pain
and his insistence that Neoptolemos acknowledge his suffering.

had enough of wandering.[69]

NEOPTOLEMOS

            Oh, you unfortunate man,
shown to be unfortunate indeed in all your toils!   760
Do you want me touch you, then, and take hold of you?

PHILOKTETES

No, no—not that! But take this bow
for me, as you asked to just now, until
the present pain of the disease subsides;   765
guard it and keep it safe. Sleep takes hold
of me, whenever this evil departs; the pain can't
stop before then, but you must let me
sleep in peace. If those men come
during this time, I urge you, by the gods,   770
don't let them have the weapons willingly or unwillingly
or in any way, lest you cause your own
death and mine, who am your suppliant.

NEOPTOLEMOS

Have courage as to my care and foresight. The bow shall not be
   given
except to you and me; hand it over, and may good luck come
   with it!   775

PHILOKTETES

There, my son, take it; and pray reverently to divine jealousy
that it not be a source of many troubles for you, as it was
for me and the one who owned it before me.[70]

---

[69] The scholiast on 758 comments that the metaphor of the "wandering disease" is appropriate to a "wild beast" (cf. 698), and Jebb, in his commentary, pp. 124-5, notes that "intermittent fevers" were called "wanderers" by medical writers.

[70] "*divine jealousy*" : it is a common notion in archaic and classical Greek texts, e.g. Pindar, *Pythian* 10.20-1; Aischylos, *Persians* 362, *Agamemnon* 904, 946-7; Euripides, *Alcestis* 1135; Herodotos, *Persian Wars*, I.32, that the gods are "jealous" and begrudge good fortune and happiness to human beings. Here possession of the bow would constitute "good fortune," and Philoktetes suggests that his sufferings and those of Herakles before him were the result of such "divine jealousy."

NEOPTOLEMOS

You gods, grant this to the two of us; and may there be
a swift and prosperous sailing to where   780
our journey is directed and a god thinks right.

PHILOKTETES

Ah, ah, ah, ah!
I fear, my child, your prayer may be unfulfilled;
for again this oozing blood drips dark-red
from the depths, and I foresee some new trouble.
Aah, alas!   785
Aah, aah my foot, what evils you cause me!
It creeps toward me,
this thing comes closer. Ah, wretched me.
You know what's happening; please don't run away!
Aah!   790
Kephallenian stranger,[71] I wish this anguish would go
right through your breast. Aah, aah!
Aah, aah again! O you two generals,
Agamemnon and Menelaos, I wish that you might feed this disease
for an equal length of time instead of me.   795
Oh!
Death, death, how is it that you can never come
though I always call you every day in this way?
My child, my noble child, take me and
burn me in this fire they call   800
"Lemnian."[72] O my noble child! I too once
thought it right to do this for the son of Zeus,
in return for these weapons that you now keep safe.
What do you say, my son?
What do you say? Why are you silent? What are you thinking,
my child?   805

NEOPTOLEMOS

I've been in pain for a long time now, grieving for your troubles.

---

[71] *"Kephallenian stranger"*: Odysseus (see on 264).

[72] *"the fire they call / Lemnian"*: "Lemnian fire" was proverbial and probably
referred to Mt. Moschylos, a well-known volcano in the eastern part of
Lemnos. Philoktetes associates the fire of this volcano with the funeral
pyre of Herakles, which he himself had kindled on Mt. Oita.

PHILOKTETES
But have courage too, my child: she
comes to me sharply and departs quickly.
I beg you, don't leave me alone!

NEOPTOLEMOS
Have courage, we will stay.

PHILOKTETES
                          You'll stay?

NEOPTOLEMOS
                                    Know this for sure.   810

PHILOKTETES
I don't ask that you swear an oath, my child.

NEOPTOLEMOS
No, it is not right for me to go without you.

PHILOKTETES
Give me your hand as a pledge.

NEOPTOLEMOS
                          I give this pledge to stay.[73]

PHILOKTETES
Up there now, there—

NEOPTOLEMOS
                          Where do you mean?

PHILOKTETES
                                         Up—

NEOPTOLEMOS
You're beside yourself, again. Why? Why do you gaze up at the
    sky?   815

PHILOKTETES
Let me go, let me go!

NEOPTOLEMOS
              Where should I let you go?

---

[73]   Giving and receiving a (right) hand is a formal gesture of friendship and
    trust. Philoktetes refers bitterly to this gesture in 942-4.

PHILOKTETES

Just let me go!

NEOPTOLEMOS
I won't!

PHILOKTETES
You'll kill me, if you touch me!

NEOPTOLEMOS
Well, then, I'm letting you go, if you're a bit more rational.

PHILOKTETES
O Earth, receive me as I die now;
this evil no longer lets me stand upright.   820

(Philoktetes collapses on the ground)

NEOPTOLEMOS
I think that sleep will take hold of this man
before too long: look how his head is nodding backwards;
yes, sweat is pouring down his whole body,
and a vein of dark blood has burst forth
from the end of his foot. Friends, let's leave   825
him in peace, so he may fall asleep.

FIRST KOMMOS

STROPHE

CHORUS
Sleep, knowing nothing of pain, Sleep, knowing nothing of sorrows,
may you come to us with a favorable breath,
my king, and bless our life; and on his eyes   830
may you keep spread this light that is spread now.[74]
Come, Healer, come to me!
My child, consider where you stand
and where you will go
and what to think of next. You see now.   835

---

[74] *"and on his eyes / ...is spread now*: i.e., may you keep him asleep. At some
points in their lyric exchange with Neoptolemos (827-64), the Chorus seem
to pity Philoktetes and wish for Sleep to heal him. Mainly, however, they
urge Neoptolemos to seize the opportunity to take the bow and leave,
in effect telling him to abandon Philoktetes as Odysseus had ten years
earlier.

Why do we wait to act?
The critical moment, decisive in all things,
very often wins triumphant victory by sudden action!

HEXAMETERS

NEOPTOLEMOS

No, this man hears nothing, but I see that we have hunted
down this bow in vain, if we sail without him.   840
The crown is his; he's the one the god said to bring.
It's an infamous shame to boast with falsehoods of things
    unaccomplished.[75]

ANTISTROPHE

CHORUS

No, my child, a god will see to this;
but however you answer me next time, speak
in a whisper, my child, a whisper of words.   845
For sick men's unsleeping sleep
can see keenly.
But whatever you can possibly do,
be sure to do it,
to do it secretly.   850
You know of whom I'm speaking:
if you hold the same thought as this man,
the sufferings to see in this are insoluble even for those who
    are subtle.[76]

EPODE

The wind, my child, the wind is yours. The   855
man cannot see, stretched out helpless
in the dark of night
(a good sleep has no fears)
with no command of hand or foot or anything,   860
like one who lies dead in Hades.
Consider, see if what you say

---

[75]   Neoptolemos chants 839-42 in dactylic hexameter, the traditional meter of
    epic poetry and divine oracles. C.H. Whitman, *Sophocles: A Study in Heroic
    Humanism* (Cambridge, MA, 1951), p. 176, calls these lines Neoptolemos'
    "first moment of conscious moral action."

[76]   The text and sense of 853-4 are uncertain.

is opportune; as far as my mind
can grasp things, the effort
that arouses no fear is most effective.

(Philoktetes begins to awaken)

NEOPTOLEMOS
I command you to be silent and keep your wits about you,   865
the man is raising his head and opening his eyes.

PHILOKTETES
O light that follows sleep, and the watch kept
by these strangers—unbelievable and more than I could hope for.
No, my son, I never would have thought that you
could stand to stay beside me, pitying   870
my troubles in this way and helping me.
The sons of Atreus could not bring themselves
to bear this so easily, those brave generals.
But your nature, my child, since it is noble
and comes from noble stock, made light of all   875
these things, though burdened with my shouting and my stench.
Now, while this trouble seems to have stopped
and forgotten about me, my child, you be the one
to lift me up, you yourself set me on my feet, my child,
so that, whenever the pain releases me,   880
we may set out for the ship and not delay our sailing.

NEOPTOLEMOS
I'm glad to see you beyond expectation
still in the light of life and breathing without pain!
To judge by the misfortunes that attend you,
your symptoms seemed like those of one no longer living.   885
Now raise yourself, or if you prefer, these men
here will carry you; they will not shrink from the task,
since you and I have decided to act in this way.

PHILOKTETES
Thank you, my son, lift me up, just as you intend,
but leave these men alone, so they are not burdened by the foul   890
smell before it is necessary; the labor of living
with me on board the ship will be enough for them!

NEOPTOLEMOS
All right; stand up and hold on to me yourself.

PHILOKTETES
Have courage; the force of habit will help me stand up straight.

NEOPTOLEMOS
Aah![77] What then should I do next after this?   895

PHILOKTETES
What is it, my son? Where is your speech wandering?

NEOPTOLEMOS
I don't know where I should turn my perplexed words.

PHILOKTETES
You perplexed? At what? Don't say this, my child.

NEOPTOLEMOS
But here I am, I've reached that point of suffering.

PHILOKTETES
The unpleasantness of the disease hasn't hit you,   900
has it, so that you won't bring me as a passenger after all?

NEOPTOLEMOS
Everything is unpleasant, when a man
abandons his own nature and does what is unfitting.

PHILOKTETES
But you do not differ from your father at all
in word or deed, by helping a good man!   905

NEOPTOLEMOS
I will appear base; this is the pain I've long been feeling.

PHILOKTETES
Not in your present actions, at least; but what you say frightens me.

---

[77]   *"Aah"* (*papai*): Neoptolemos' *papai* indicates that he feels emotional distress
analogous to the physical pain that leads Philoktetes to utter the same
sound at 745-6, 785-6, 790, and 792-3. His helplessness culminates in his "O
Zeus, what should I do?" (908), suggesting that, by a kind of role reversal,
he is as much in need of ethical salvation as Philoktetes is of physical
deliverance. Neoptolemos suffers from *aporia*, "distress at being perplexed"
(*aporon...epos*, 897; *aporeis...*, 898), similar to the *aporia* experienced by
Socrates' interlocutors in a number of Platonic dialogues, when they are
forced to give up their previous convictions and assumptions and admit
their ignorance.

NEOPTOLEMOS

O Zeus, what should I do? Will I be found worthless a second time,
hiding what I must not hide and speaking the most shameful of
words?

PHILOKTETES

Unless my judgment is bad, this man seems likely   910
to betray me and sail away, leaving me behind.

NEOPTOLEMOS

No, not I, I will not leave you, but I may send you
on a painful voyage—this is the pain I've long been feeling.

PHILOKTETES

What do you mean, my child? I don't understand.

NEOPTOLEMOS

I will conceal nothing from you: you must sail to Troy,   915
to the Achaians and the army of the sons of Atreus.

PHILOKTETES

What did you say?

NEOPTOLEMOS

                            Don't groan before you understand.

PHILOKTETES

Understand what? What are you planning to do to me?

NEOPTOLEMOS

In the first place, to save you from this trouble, and then
to go with you and sack the plain of Troy.   920

PHILOKTETES

Do you really plan to do this?

NEOPTOLEMOS

                            A great necessity
compels these things; don't be angry, when you hear of it.

PHILOKTETES

I'm lost, wretch that I am, betrayed; stranger, what
have you done to me?[78] Return my bow at once!

---

[78] "*stranger, what / have you done to me?*": Philoktetes, who has been calling
Neoptolemos "my son" and "my child," is led by his betrayal to refer to
him once again as "stranger."

NEOPTOLEMOS

No, it's not possible: both what is right and   925
what is expedient make me heed those in authority.

PHILOKTETES

You fire, you utter monster and most hateful
contrivance of terrible villainy,[79] how you've treated me,
how you've deceived me! Aren't you ashamed to look
at me, the suppliant who turned to you, you wretch?   930
You've taken my bow and robbed me of my life.
Return it, I beseech you; return it, I beg you, my child!
By the gods of your fathers, don't take away my life!
Wretched me! No, he won't even speak to me any more,
but looks away like this, as if he will never let it go.   935
You harbors, you headlands, you communities of
mountain beasts, you steep rocks—I make
this lament to you, my usual companions,
since I know of no one else to whom I might speak.[80]
How he treated me, the son of Achilles! He swore   940
to bring me back home, but he is taking me to Troy;
he gave his right hand as a pledge, but he took and
keeps my bow, the sacred bow of Herakles, the son of Zeus,

---

[79]   *"You fire, you utter monster...."*: Neoptolemos remains silent throughout
        Philoktetes' emotionally charged speech (927-62), ignoring questions and
        exclamations that invite his response at the end of 930, 932, 933, 935, 950,
        and 962, and perhaps most strongly within 951. He speaks only when
        directly asked by the Chorus, "What should we do?" Perhaps, though, some
        physical gestures by Neoptolemos as Philoktetes speaks might indicate
        the development within him of the pity he finally voices in 965-6 and the
        burdensome helplessness that he acknowledges in 969-70.

[80]   In their entry song, the Chorus sing pityingly of how Philoktetes "lies
        alone...apart from others / with the shaggy or dappled / wild beasts...,"
        hearing only the echo of his own "bitter cries of sorrow" (182-90). Philoktetes,
        too, speaks of the island in terms of his solitude and painful helplessness
        (300-13). Now that he has been betrayed by Neoptolemos and robbed of
        his bow, Philoktetes addresses the natural elements of the island (harbors,
        cliffs, mountain beasts, birds flying overhead) with increased frequency and
        with a feeling of solidarity, as if, harsh and threatening though they may
        be, they are his true companions (e.g. 936ff., 1081ff., 1146ff.). Only at the
        end of the play, when he is ready to leave the island, does he "call upon"
        the "house that kept watch with me," the waters, mountains, and winds,
        and the "sea-surrounded land of Lemnos" as beneficent (1452-64).

and says that he will show it off to the Argives.
He takes me by force, as if he had caught a strong man,   945
and doesn't know that he is killing a corpse, or the shadow of smoke,
a phantom merely.[81] He wouldn't have taken me in my strength,
or even as I am, except by treachery.
Now I have been deceived, ill-fated as I am. So what should I do?
No, give it back! No, even now, be yourself!   950
What do you say? You're silent. Ill-fated as I am, I am nothing!
You rock with two entrances, I'll return
to you again—but naked, without the means to live.
I'll wither away in this dwelling, alone,
slaying no winged bird, no mountain beast   955
with this bow; rather I myself, in my misery,
will die and furnish a feast for those off whom I used to feed,
and those whom I once hunted will now hunt me.
Wretched me, I will pay blood for blood in reprisal,
a victim of the man who seemed to know no evil.   960
May you perish—but not yet, until I learn if you will change
your mind again; if not, may you die foully!

CHORUS
What should we do? It's your decision, my king,
whether we sail or comply with this man's words.

NEOPTOLEMOS
A strange pity for this man has taken hold of me,   965
not for the first time now, but long since.

PHILOKTETES
Have pity, my child, by the gods; don't expose yourself
to reproach by mortals for deceiving and robbing me.

---

81   Philoktetes several times refers to himself metaphorically as "dead": "a
      corpse" (946); "a corpse among the living" (1018); "I'm nothing and
      have long been dead, as far as you're concerned" (1030). In effect, while
      abandoned on "sea-surrounded" Lemnos " (1, 1464), he is unable to function
      as he normally would—as a warrior hero—and thus is symbolically dead.
      Philoktetes is, as it were, restored to life when he is able to leave the island
      for a "return home" (*nostos*, 1471) to health and heroic glory at Troy. In
      this way he resembles Odysseus in the *Odyssey*, who is functionally and
      symbolically dead on "sea-surrounded" Ogygia, the island of Kalypso (*Od.*
      1.50, 198), but survives to return home and, by killing the Suitors, restores
      his heroic identity as husband, father, and king.

NEOPTOLEMOS

Alas, what should I do? I wish I'd never left
Skyros, I'm so burdened by the present situation.   970

PHILOKTETES

You are not evil, but you seem to have come here after learning
shameful things from evil men. Now leave these shameful things to
    others
for whom they are fitting, and set sail, once you've given me back
    my arms.

NEOPTOLEMOS

What should we do, men?

(Odysseus springs from ambush, accompanied by some sailors)

ODYSSEUS

                          What should you *do*, you worst of men?[82]
Will you not surrender this bow to me again?   975

PHILOKTETES

Alas, who is this man? Do I hear Odysseus?

ODYSSEUS

Yes, be sure of it, Odysseus, whom you see before you in person!

PHILOKTETES

Alas, I've been sold and destroyed! So this was
the man who caught me and deprived me of my arms.

ODYSSEUS

It was I, be sure of it, and no one else; I admit it.   980

PHILOKTETES

Return the bow, my son, let me have it!

ODYSSEUS

                              That
he will never do, even if he wants to; and you too must
come along with us, or they'll convey you by force.

---

[82] *What should you* do, *you worst of men?"*: as Neoptolemos once again expresses
     his ethical helplessness, Odysseus enters suddenly in the middle of the
     line, surprising the audience as well as Neoptolemos and Philoktetes.
     Odysseus makes a similarly sudden entrance between 1292 and 1293 in
     an unsuccessful attempt to prevent Neoptolemos from returning the bow
     to Philoktetes.

PHILOKTETES
Me, you basest and boldest of evil men,
these men will bring me by force?

ODYSSEUS
                              If you don't come willingly.   985

PHILOKTETES
O Lemnian land and you, all-conquering flame
kindled by Hephaistos,[83] is it really to be borne
that this man will bring me by force from your realm?

ODYSSEUS
It is Zeus, you should know, Zeus who rules this land,
Zeus who has decided this; I am his servant.   990

PHILOKTETES
You hateful creature, what things you find to say!
Offering the gods as a pretext, you make these gods false!

ODYSSEUS
No, I make them true. And the road must be traveled.

PHILOKTETES
I say, "No!"

ODYSSEUS
                              But I say, "Yes!" There must be obedience in this.[84]

PHILOKTETES
Alas for wretched me! Clearly my father   995
sired me as a slave, not a free man!

ODYSSEUS
No, as an equal to the best men, with whom
you must take Troy and raze it to the ground.

---

[83] *"all-conquering flame / kindled by Hephaistos*: the flame Hephaistos causes to
     erupt from the volcano Moschylos. Lemnos was sacred to Hephaistos, and
     at *Odyssey* 8.284 it is called "by far the dearest of lands" to him. He refers
     in *Iliad* 1.593 to his landing there, when Zeus hurled him from Olympos
     for taking Hera's part in a quarrel. The scholiast on 986 comments that the
     god's workshops were said to be on Lemnos.

[84] *"The road must be traveled....There must be obedience....":* In the Greek,
     Odysseus speaks impersonally, in terms of necessity, as he and Neoptolemos
     do elsewhere in the play, both to assert their authority and to evade personal
     responsibility for their actions.

PHILOKTETES

No, never, not even if I must suffer every evil,
at least not while I have this steep precipice before me.   1000

ODYSSEUS

What do you mean?

PHILOKTETES

             I'll throw myself at once from this rock,
and smash this head of mine on the rock below.

ODYSSEUS

Two of you, seize him! Don't let him do this!

(Two sailors seize Philoktetes from either side.)

PHILOKTETES

My hands, hunted down and caught by this man,
how you suffer without your dear bow.   1005

(To Odysseus)

You who think no clean or generous thought—
you stole upon me again and hunted me down, using
as your screen this boy who was unknown to me—
a boy too good for you, but worthy of me,
who knew nothing except to follow orders,   1010
and now is clearly pained by what
he himself did wrong and what I suffered.
But your evil mind, always on the lookout
from its secret places, taught him well, though he
was by nature unapt and unwilling, to be clever in evil.   1015
And now, you wretch, you intend to bind me and take me away
from this shore where you cast me out without a friend,
deserted, with no community, a corpse among the living.
Alas!
May you perish! And yet I've often prayed for this,
but since the gods grant me nothing sweet,   1020
you still are enjoying life, while I am in pain
from the very fact that I live wretchedly, with many troubles,
laughed at by you and the sons of Atreus,

those two generals, whom you serve in this matter.[85]
Yet you sailed with them under compulsion,   1025
after being tricked,[86] while I, utter wretch that I am,
who sailed voluntarily with my seven ships,
was dishonorably cast out—by them, as you would say, but
  they say you did it.
Why are you taking me now? Why are you taking me away?
  For what?
I'm nothing and have long been dead, as far as you're
  concerned.   1030
You whom the gods hate most, how am I now not lame,
not foul-smelling? How can you burn sacred offerings
if I sail with you, how can you still pour libations?
This was your excuse for throwing me out.
May you perish miserably! And you shall perish   1035
for the wrong you've done me, if the gods care about justice.
And I know they do care: for you would never have set sail
on this voyage for the sake of a wretched man like me,
unless some divine goad had led you to do so.
Land of my fathers, and you gods who watch over it,   1040
if you pity me in any way, punish them,
punish them all, no matter how long it takes!
Though I live pitiably, if I could see them ruined,
I'd think I had escaped from my disease.

CHORUS

The stranger is bitter, Odysseus, and has spoken   1045
this bitter speech that does not give in to troubles.

ODYSSEUS

I could say many things in response to this man's words,
if time permitted; as it is, I limit myself to saying just one thing:
where there's a need for such men, such a man am I;

---

85   *"those two generals, whom you serve..."*: Odysseus had claimed earlier to
     be serving Zeus (989-90), but Philoktetes considers him either an ignoble
     lackey of Agamemnon and Menelaos or, if "whom you serve" is ironic, one
     who falsely claims to be just following orders.

86   Odysseus tried to avoid going to Troy by pretending to be mad. His ruse
     was exposed by Palamedes, and he was compelled to join the expedition.
     The story was told in the *Kypria* and dramatized by Sophokles in his *Madness
     of Odysseus*, which is not extant.

and wherever there's a competition of just and good men,   1050
you would find no one more pious than I.
My nature is to desire victory in all things[87]—
except in your case; to you I shall now give way willingly.
Yes, leave him alone, don't touch him any more!
Let him stay here! We have no further need of you,   1055
now that we have these weapons: Teukros
knows how to use them,[88] and I think
that I could control these weapons no worse
than you, and with my hand shoot no less straight.
Why do we need you, then? Farewell, and enjoy walking around
      your Lemnos.[89]   1060
Let's go; perhaps your special reward and privilege
will confer honor on me, the honor that should be yours.

PHILOKTETES
Oh, what should I do, ill fated as I am? Will you
appear among the Argives adorned with my weapons?

ODYSSEUS
Don't speak to me any more, since I'm on my way.   1065

PHILOKTETES
Seed of Achilles, will I no longer hear
your voice either; will you go away like this?

ODYSSEUS
Come on, you; don't keep looking at him, noble though you are,
so you won't ruin our good fortune!

PHILOKTETES
Strangers, will you really leave me behind alone   1070

---

[87]   This is the clearest expression in the play of Odysseus' shifty nature and
    Sophistic moral relativism. The word "such" (*toioutos*) is unstable and
    changes its meaning at different times and in different circumstances.
    It expresses how Odysseus opportunistically changes himself, adopting
    whatever values will bring him victory at any given moment.

[88]   In the *Iliad*, Teukros, the half-brother of Ajax, son of Telamon, is an
    outstanding archer on the Greek side. In Sophokles' *Ajax*, with the support
    of Odysseus, he successfully opposes Agamemnon and Menelaos to achieve
    the burial of his brother.

[89]   Odysseus cruelly mocks Philoktetes, who of course can hardly "walk" at all
    (cf. 290-2, 294).

in this way? Won't you take pity on me?

CHORUS
This boy is our commander. Whatever
he may say to you, that's what we say too.

NEOPTOLEMOS
I'll hear from this man that I am by nature
full of pity; but all the same, stay, if that's what he wants,   1075
for as long as it takes the sailors to prepare
things on board and for us to pray to the gods.
Perhaps he will come to think better of us
during this time. (*to Odysseus*) Let's go, then, the two of us,[90]
and you men, when we call, set forth quickly.   1080

(Exit Odysseus and Neoptolemos)

SECOND KOMMOS [cf. line 827/8]

STROPHE A

PHILOKTETES
You hollow of cavernous rock,
hot and ice cold by turns,
so I wasn't, after all, ever going
to leave you, wretched me, but you
will be my witness, even as I am dying.   1085
Alas, alas!
You wretched dwelling,
so full of my pain,
what now will be my daily portion?
What hope of food will I chance on—and from where—   1090
wretched as I am?
You birds on high, who once feared my twanging bowstring,
   come;
I no longer have the means to hit you.

CHORUS
It was you, heavy-doomed man, you who brought it about;   1095

---

90   Neoptolemos use of the dual (see on 25) expresses his solidarity with
     Odysseus, despite his earlier protestations of friendship with Philoktetes,
     and despite Philoktetes' appeal (1066-67).

this fortune does not come from elsewhere, from something
   greater.
When it was possible for you to think rationally,
you chose to embrace the worse, not the better destiny.   1100

ANTISTROPHE A

PHILOKTETES
I am wretched, wretched after all,
and abused by my suffering, I
who now will perish,
dwelling here from now on
with no companion, wretched me,   1105
alas, alas,
no longer bringing in food,
no longer getting it with powerful hands
from my winged weapons.   1110
The unlooked-for, deceitful
words of a treacherous mind fooled me.
I wish I could see him,
the man who plotted these things, with my pain as his portion
for an equal length of time!   1115

CHORUS
The gods' doom did this to you, not treachery
by my hand; aim your hateful,
ill-fated curse at others.   1120
For this is my concern, that you not reject my friendship.

STROPHE B

PHILOKTETES
Alas—sitting somewhere
on the shore of the gray sea,
he laughs at me, brandishing in his hand   1125
the arms that sustained my wretched life,
which no one ever handled.
You dear bow, violently
forced from hands dear to you,
surely you see with pity, if you have   1130
any feeling, that Herakles'
wretched comrade
will no longer use you in the future;

instead, you are handled
by a man of many devices,   1135
seeing the shameful deceptions
of the hated enemy,
who devised against us countless evils
sprung from shameful deeds.

CHORUS
It is a man's part to assert his own right,   1140
but not, once he has spoken, to sting
with a rancorous and painful tongue.
That man, but one out of many,
at this man's command,[91]
accomplished a public benefit for his friends.   1145

ANTISTROPHE B

PHILOKTETES
My winged prey, and you tribes
of wild beasts with flashing eyes
who inhabit these mountain pastures,
no longer will you rush in flight
from your lairs, for my two hands lack   1150
my arrows' former strength;
oh, I am miserable now!
No, move freely; here I am, held back
by my lameness, no longer the object
of your fear; now it is fine   1155
to take revenge as you please and glut
your mouths on my gleaming flesh.
I shall leave life behind at once; for
where will I find a means to live?
Who can feed thus on the winds,   1160
no longer controlling anything
that the life-giving earth sends forth?

CHORUS
By the gods, if you have any respect for a friend,
who approaches you with all good will, draw near!

---

[91] "this man's": Agamemnon's

Know well, know, it is in your power   1165
to escape this deadly doom.
It is pitiable to feed it with your flesh, and no one
with whom it dwells can learn to bear its countless burdens.

NON-CORRESPONDING SONG

PHILOKTETES

Again, again you remind me of my
old pain, though you're the best   1170
of those who have been here before.
What have you done to me? Why did you destroy me?

CHORUS

What do you mean?

PHILOKTETES

If you expected
to bring me to the land of Troy that I detest.   1175

CHORUS

Yes, I think this is best.

PHILOKTETES

Then leave me alone now!

CHORUS

Your command is welcome to me, welcome, and one I do
willingly.
Let's go, let's go
to our various stations on the ship.   1180

PHILOKTETES

Don't, by Zeus who hears curses, I beg you,
don't go!

CHORUS

Be calm!

PHILOKTETES

Strangers,
by the gods, stay!

CHORUS

Why are you shouting?   1185

PHILOKTETES
Woe, woe,
my destiny, my destiny; I am lost, wretched me.
Foot, foot—what shall I do with you in the future,
for the rest of my life, wretched me?
Strangers, come back again! 1190

CHORUS
For what? Your thought
is utterly different from what you previously indicated.[92]

PHILOKTETES
It's nothing to be angry at,
if a man crazed by a storm
of grief should cry out madly. 1195

CHORUS
Come now, you wretched man, as we bid you.

PHILOKTETES
Never, never—know that this is firm,
not even if the fire-bearing lord of lightning is going
to burn me in a blaze of lightning and thunder.
May Ilion perish and all those beneath it, 1200
all who had the heart to reject
this poor, lame foot of mine.
Strangers, grant me one prayer at least!

CHORUS
What do you want?

PHILOKTETES
A sword, if there is one somewhere,
pass it forward to me, or an axe, or any weapon! 1205

CHORUS
So you can do what violent deed?

PHILOKTETES
So I can cut off my head and all my limbs with my own hand!
My mind is bent on slaughter, slaughter!

---

[92] He had told them to leave in 1177.

CHORUS
Why?

PHILOKTETES
   To seek my father.   1210

CHORUS
Where in the world?

PHILOKTETES
      In Hades!
For he no longer sees the light of life.[93]
My city, my native city,
how I wish I could I see you,
wretch that I am, I
who left behind your sacred stream   1215
and went to help the hated
Danaans. Now I am nothing.

CHORUS
I would have left you long ago and been
approaching my ship by now, if we did not see
Odysseus on his way here and the offspring   1220
of Achilles also approaching toward us.

(Exit Philoktetes into the cave. Enter Neoptolemos followed by Odysseus.)

ODYSSEUS
Won't you say why you're turning back now
and moving swiftly in such great haste?

NEOPTOLEMOS
To undo the mistake I made earlier.

ODYSSEUS
You speak strangely. What was your mistake?   1225

NEOPTOLEMOS
The one I made by obeying you and the whole army—

---

[93] In his despair, Philoktetes thinks of his father as dead. Earlier, when he
  was more optimistic, he thought of him as still alive (492-99), and later he
  will do so again (1371).

ODYSSEUS
What did you do that was not fitting?

NEOPTOLEMOS
taking a man by treachery and shameful deception.

ODYSSEUS
What man? You're not planning something new, are you?

NEOPTOLEMOS
Nothing new, but to the son of Poias—   1230

ODYSSEUS
What will you do? A strange fear has come over me.

NEOPTOLEMOS
from whom I got this bow, to him again—

ODYSSEUS
Zeus, what do you mean? Surely you don't plan to give it back?

NEOPTOLEMOS
Yes, I do, for I've taken it shamefully and unjustly.

ODYSSEUS
By the gods, do you say this to mock me?   1235

NEOPTOLEMOS
If it's mockery to speak the truth.

ODYSSEUS
What do you mean, son of Achilles? What did you say?

NEOPTOLEMOS
Do you want me to go over the same ground in the same words,
two and three times?

ODYSSEUS
I would have wished not to hear them even once, to begin with.

NEOPTOLEMOS
Be sure now, you've heard all I have to say.   1240

ODYSSEUS
There's someone—there is—who will stop you from doing this.

NEOPTOLEMOS
What do you mean? Who will be the one to stop me?

ODYSSEUS
The whole army of the Achaians, including myself.

NEOPTOLEMOS
You are clever by nature, but what you say is not at all clever.

ODYSSEUS
Neither what you say nor what you would do is clever.   1245

NEOPTOLEMOS
But if it's just, that's better and worth more than clever.

ODYSSEUS
How is it just to surrender what you got
by my plans?

NEOPTOLEMOS
                    I'll try to retrieve
the shameful mistake I committed.

ODYSSEUS
In doing this, are you not afraid of the army of the Achaians?   1250

NEOPTOLEMOS
With justice on my side, I'm not afraid of your army.

ODYSSEUS
You ought to be afraid, for we'll compel you by force.[94]

NEOPTOLEMOS
No, I will not obey the force of your hand and do as you say.

ODYSSEUS
Then we'll fight not with the Trojans, but with you.

NEOPTOLEMOS
Let what will be, be.

ODYSSEUS
                    Do you see my right hand
touching the hilt of my sword?

NEOPTOLEMOS
                              You'll see me too   1255
doing this same thing, without further delay.

---

[94]   The text is uncertain. A line is probably missing from the manuscripts on
which all modern texts of *Philoktetes* are based.

ODYSSEUS
Well, I'll leave you alone, but when I arrive,
I'll tell this to the whole army, which will punish you.

(Exit Odysseus; Neoptolemos calls after him as he departs.)

NEOPTOLEMOS
You're being prudent; and if you're reasonable in this way
    from now on,
perhaps you could keep clear of trouble.   1260

(turning to the cave)

Son of Poias, I mean you, Philoktetes,
leave your rocky dwelling and come out.

PHILOKTETES
Now what noisy cry rises beside my cave?
Why do you call for me? What do you want, strangers?
Oh, it's something bad. Are you here to usher in   1265
some great trouble for me, on top of my other troubles?

NEOPTOLEMOS
Have courage, and hear what I've come to tell you.

PHILOKTETES
I'm afraid, since I suffered before from fine
words, when I was persuaded by what you said.

NEOPTOLEMOS
Isn't it possible to change my mind again?   1270

PHILOKTETES
That's how you were with words, when you stole
the bow from me—trustworthy, but secretly fatal.

NEOPTOLEMOS
But not now! I want to hear from you
whether you've decided to stay here and endure
or to sail with us.

PHILOKTETES
                          Stop, not another word;   1275
all that you say will be said in vain.

NEOPTOLEMOS
This is what you've decided?

PHILOKTETES

                Yes, believe me, more firmly than I can say.

NEOPTOLEMOS

Well, I would have wished that you had been persuaded
by my words; but if I can't speak opportunely and effectively,
I'm finished.

PHILOKTETES

             Yes, you will say everything in vain,   1280
and you'll never have my mind's good will,
you who treacherously took my means of life
and have robbed me of it.[95] Then you come
to speak sense to me, you most hateful offspring of a noble father.
May you perish—the sons of Atreus, most of all, then   1285
   the son of Laertes, and you!

NEOPTOLEMOS

                  Stop cursing me,
and receive these weapons from my hand.

PHILOKTETES

What did you say? Are we being tricked a second time?

NEOPTOLEMOS

No, I swear by the pure majesty of highest Zeus.

PHILOKTETES

You've said the friendliest words, if you speak truly!   1290

NEOPTOLEMOS

The deed will make it clear. Come, reach out
your right hand and be master of your weapons.

(While Philoktetes reaches for the bow, Odysseus enters unexpectedly)

ODYSSEUS

No, I forbid it, as the gods are witnesses,
on behalf of the sons of Atreus and the whole army.

PHILOKTETES

My child, whose voice is that? Did I hear   1295
Odysseus?

---

[95] *"means of life"*: Philoktetes puns on *bíos* ("life," "means of life") and *biós* ("bow").

ODYSSEUS

Be sure of it! And you see me near by,
the man who'll convey you to the plain of Troy by force,
whether or not the son of Achilles is willing.

(Philoktetes aims an arrow at Odysseus)

PHILOKTETES

To your own sorrow, if this arrow goes straight.

(Neoptolemos seizes Philoktetes' arm)

NEOPTOLEMOS

No, don't, by the gods, don't shoot the arrow.   1300

PHILOKTETES

By the gods, let go of my hand, my dearest child.

NEOPTOLEMOS

I won't let go. *(Exit Odysseus)*[96]

PHILOKTETES

Alas, why did you stop me from killing
with my bow a man who is my hated enemy?

NEOPTOLEMOS

No, this would be good for neither you nor me.

PHILOKTETES

Then know this much, at least: the leaders of the army,   1305
the lying heralds of the Achaians, are cowards
in battle, although they are bold with words.[97]

NEOPTOLEMOS

Well, now you have the bow, and there's no reason
for you to be angry with me or blame me.

PHILOKTETES

I agree. You've shown your nature, my child, the stock   1310
from which you were born—not from Sisyphos as a father

---

[96] *Exit Odysseus*: Odysseus' brief appearance of under ten lines, the shortest
      by any major character in extant Attic tragedy, signals the futility of his
      merely verbal courage.

[97] *"lying heralds"*: "In Attic Tragedy the herald was especially associated with
      unsuccessful bluster." (Jebb, p. 201)

but from Achilles who, when he was alive,
had the greatest glory, as he now does among the dead.

NEOPTOLEMOS

I'm glad that you speak well of my father
and myself; now hear what I desire to get   1315
from you.   Human beings must bear
the fortunes they are given by the gods,
but those who cling to self-inflicted harm,
as you do—it's not right for anyone
either to pity or to pardon them.   1320
You have become savage, and you don't accept advice; if anyone
tries to put sense in your head, speaking with good will,
you hate him and consider him an enemy who wishes you ill.
Nevertheless I will speak, and I call on Zeus who witnesses oaths.
Know this and inscribe it in your mind: 1325
you are sick with this pain by divine fortune,[98]
since you approached the guardian of Chrysê, the hidden,
indwelling serpent that guards the roofless shrine.[99]
Know too that you will never find relief from this
heavy sickness, while the same sun   1330
rises in the east and sets again in the west,
until you yourself come willingly to the plain of Troy

---

[98]   "*divine fortune*": "fortune" (*tychê*) usually suggests something that happens randomly, at least from a human point of view (e.g. 546). When it is called "divine" or is said to have been sent by "the gods" (1316-7) or by a particular god (e.g. Euripides, *Hippolytus 371*, *Herakles* 1393), it is an open question whether "fortune" and divinity should be thought of as moral or amoral. Often "divine" or "by the gods" means only that the speaker can imagine no other explanation for some extraordinary occurrence or sequence of events. Beginning in the late fifth century,"fortune" is sometimes separated from the gods and itself deified (e.g. *Oedipus the King* 1080). The moral relevance of divinity is a major question throughout *Philoktetes*: cf. 8-9, 191-200, 315-6, 451-2, 610-13, 1036-39, 1338-41, 1440-44.

[99]   In describing the snake that bit Philoktetes, Neoptolomos uses a technical term for the sacred serpent dwelling in the Erechtheum, the temple of *Athena Polias* ("Athena the City-Goddess") on the Athenian acropolis. This serpent, which represented the mythical King Erichthonios, guarded the temple. (Cf. Aristophanes, *Lysistrata* 759, Herodotos 8.41, Pausanias I.24.7.) See on 134.

and meet the sons of Asklepios who are with us.[100]
Then you will be eased from the burden of this sickness, and
  with this bow—
and with me—you will shine forth as the conqueror of the
  Trojan towers.   1335
I'll tell you how I know that this is so.
There is a man among us, a Trojan captive,
Helenos, the best of seers, who says clearly
that this must happen; and further, in addition,
that Troy must be utterly destroyed   1340
within the present summer, or he willingly surrenders
himself for us to kill, if he speaks these things falsely.[101]
So since you know this, give your agreement willingly.
It's a fine addition for you, to be judged the single
best man among the Hellenes—first to come   1345
into healing hands, and then to take Troy,
the cause of much mourning, and win the highest glory.

PHILOKTETES

O hateful life, why do you still keep me here above,
in the light of life; why do you not send me to the house of
  Hades?
Ah me, what should I do? How can I mistrust the words   1350
of this man who advises me with good will?
But should I give way, then? How, if I do this, ill-fated as
  I am,
will I come into anyone's sight? Who would speak to me?
You eyes that have seen everything done to me,
how will you endure this—that I associate   1355
with the sons of Atreus who destroyed me?
How with the accursed son of Laertes?
It is not the pain of past events that gnaws at me,

---

[100] "*sons of Asklepios*": in the *Iliad*, Machaon and Podaleirios, the sons of
  Asklepios, the god of medicine, fight on the Greek side and also serve
  as physicians. In 1437-38, Herakles promises to send Asklepios himself
  to heal Philoktetes; in the *Little Iliad*, the epic following the *Iliad* and the
  Aithopis in the "Epic Cycle," Machaon did so, without Podaleirios. See
  below, Interpretive Essay, p. 89, n. 2.

[101] On the varying terms of the prophecy, see on 610-13. It is impossible to
  know what Philoktetes thinks about the conflicting accounts of Helenos'
  words.

but I seem to foresee the sort of things I still
must suffer at their hands. When men's thought becomes   1360
the mother of evils for them, it also teaches them to be evil
in other ways. I have been wondering at you too, in this respect:
you should never be going to Troy yourself, and you should
stop me from doing so. These men violated you outrageously,
stripping you of your father's special honor. After this,   1365
will you fight as their ally and compel me to do this too?[102]
No, my child, don't, but as you swore to me,
escort me home,[103] and stay in Skyros yourself,
and leave these evil men to perish evilly.
This way you'll gain a double thanks from me   1370
and double from my father,[104] and you won't seem, by helping
evil men, to be similar in your nature to the evil ones.

NEOPTOLEMOS
What you say is reasonable, but all the same I wish
you would trust both the gods and my words,
and sail off from this land with me who am your friend.   1375

PHILOKTETES
Sail to the plain of Troy and to the most hateful
son of Atreus—with this wretched foot?

NEOPTOLEMOS
No, to those who will free you and this rotten foot of yours
from pain and save you from your disease.

PHILOKTETES
What do you mean by giving this terrible advice?   1380

---

[102]   Neoptolemos' lie about being robbed of his father's armor by Odysseus
(364-81) remains uncorrected, both when Philoktetes refers to it in 1364-66
and through the end of the play.

[103]   Neoptolemos did not actually promise to take Philoktetes home to Malis,
though Philoktetes claims here and at 1398 that he did. Perhaps Philoktetes
is conflating in his own mind Neoptolemos' promise to stay with him
while he sleeps off his paroxysm, when he takes his right hand in a formal
gesture of friendship (813), with his earlier, equivocally phrased agreement
to take him where he wants to go (526-29). In the end, however (1402),
Neoptolemos is persuaded to act on this supposed promise.

[104]   In his relative optimism, Philoktetes again thinks of his father as still alive.
See on 1212.

NEOPTOLEMOS

What I see is best for both you and me, if it's accomplished.

PHILOKTETES

Aren't you ashamed before the gods to say this?

NEOPTOLEMOS

No, why should one be ashamed of helping friends?

PHILOKTETES

Do you mean helping the sons of Atreus or helping me?

NEOPTOLEMOS

You, of course, since I'm your friend; and what I say is
friendly, too.   1385

PHILOKTETES

How can that be, when you wish to hand me over to my
enemies?

NEOPTOLEMOS

Sir, teach yourself not to be bold and arrogant in your
misfortunes.

PHILOKTETES

You will destroy me by these words, I know you will.

NEOPTOLEMOS

No, not I. I'm telling you, you don't understand.

PHILOKTETES

Don't I know that the sons of Atreus cast me away?   1390

NEOPTOLEMOS

What if, having cast you out, they will take you back and
save you?

PHILOKTETES

Never, if I must be willing to see Troy.

NEOPTOLEMOS

What, then, should we do, if my words can't
persuade you of anything I'm saying?
It's time for me to stop talking, and for you   1395
to go on living as you've been living, without salvation.

PHILOKTETES

Let me suffer what I must suffer,

but do what you promised, when you touched my right hand,
to send me home. Do this for me, child,
and don't keep putting it off;   and don't mention   1400
Troy again. As far as I'm concerned, there's been enough talking.

TROCHAIC TETRAMETERS CATALECTIC

NEOPTOLEMOS
If this is your decision, let's set forth.

PHILOKTETES
                              Oh, you have spoken a noble
                         word![105]

NEOPTOLEMOS
Now lean your step against mine.

PHILOKTETES
                              Yes, as much as I have strength
                         to.

NEOPTOLEMOS
But how shall I escape blame from the Achaians?

PHILOKTETES
                                   Don't think about it.

NEOPTOLEMOS
But I do think about it;   what if they attack my country?

PHILOKTETES
                                   I'll be present and—
                                                            1405

NEOPTOLEMOS
What will you do to help me?

---

[105] At the moment when Neoptolemos is persuaded to live up to a promise that
he never actually made (cf. his words at 526-29, 812-13, with 1367-8n.) and
the two men set out for the ship, the meter shifts suddenly and dramatically
from iambic trimeter, the normal meter of dialogue, to trochaic tetrameter
catalectic, another spoken meter that has not been used up to this point in the
play. In the Greek, the first line in this meter, 1402, expresses Neoptolemos'
troubled ambivalence at having to live up to his inherent nobility not only
by being divided between two speakers, but by the metrical anomaly of
there not being word-end after the eighth element of the line—an anomaly
that is unparalleled in extant Attic tragedy.

PHILOKTETES

...with the shafts of Herakles—

NEOPTOLEMOS
What do you mean?

PHILOKTETES

...I'll stop them from approaching your native
land.

NEOPTOLEMOS

If only
you'll do this, as you say! Now set forth, once you have kissed the
ground farewell.

*(Herakles suddenly appears above them as a god. Chanting anapests, he moves
forward on the roof of the stage building, until he reaches the position from which
he speaks to Philoktetes and Neoptolemos in iambic trimeters.)*

ANAPESTS

HERAKLES
Not yet, until you hear
our words, son of Poias;   1410
understand that you hear the voice of Herakles
in your ears and see his visible form.
I've come for your sake, leaving
my heavenly seat,
to tell of Zeus' plans for you,   1415
and to prevent the journey on which you are embarking.
Now hear my authoritative words.

IAMBIC TRIMETERS

First of all, I'll tell you of my fortunes,
how many labors I went through and labored at
to win undying glory, as you can see.   1420
Be certain that to you too it is owed to suffer this—
to make your life glorious after and through these labors.
When you go with this man to the Trojan citadel,
first you shall be freed from your terrible sickness,
and after being judged best in the army for heroism,   1425
with my bow you will end the life of Paris,
whose birth was the cause of these troubles.
You will sack Troy and, receiving the army's

greatest prize of valor, you will carry the spoils home to your halls,
to the height of Oita, your native land, for your father, Poias.   1430
But whatever spoils you take from the army,
bring to my pyre as memorials to my bow.[106]
To you, son of Achilles, I give the same
advice. You don't have the strength to take the plain of Troy
without this man, nor does he without you;   1435
but like two lions pasturing together, the two of you keep guard,
you of him and he of you.[107] I'll send
Asklepios to Ilion as healer of your disease,
since it is destined that the city be taken a second time
by my bow. And keep this in mind, when   1440
you sack the land, to be pious in things having to do with the gods:
father Zeus considers everything else secondary.
Piety does not die along with mortals;
among the living and the dead it does not perish.[108]

---

[106]   Herakles speaks of two kinds of spoils: the special ones that Philoktetes
will receive as the "greatest prize of valor" for his actions during the sack
of Troy, and the ordinary ones that he, like other warriors, will receive in
the general division of the army's booty. He is to give the former to his
father and dedicate the latter to Herakles. It was normal for Greek armies
to offer (a portion of) their spoils to the gods in gratitude for a victory.

[107]   This simile, the final instance of dual forms in the play, seems to signal the
ultimate defeat of Odysseus' effort in the Prologue to pair Neoptolemos
with himself (cf. on 25, 133). On the other hand, the simile recalls *Iliad*
10.297, where Odysseus and Diomedes go "like two lions through the dark
night" on the spying expedition during which they capture, deceive, and
butcher the Trojan spy, Dolon, then proceed to slaughter the sleeping Rhesos
and his men and steal his horses. Thus, even in a passage that appears to
present Neoptolemos, together with Philoktetes, in a favorable light, he
does not entirely escape an association with the ethically ambiguous and
unsavory Odysseus.

[108]   There is a clear allusion in 1440-44 to Neoptolemos' well-known *impiety*
during the sack of Troy, when he butchered Priam on the altar of Zeus.
This suggests that Neoptolemos will fall from the standard of nobility
that he reaches when he atones for helping Odysseus to steal the bow
by returning it to Philoktetes. Sophokles similarly (and problematically)
points beyond the ending of the play in *Elektra* 1497-98, where Aigisthos
asks if "this palace must see / the present and future troubles of the sons of
Pelops," and at *Oidipous at Kolonos* 1769-72, where Antigone tells Theseus
to send her to Thebes, "if somehow we might prevent the coming slaughter
for our blood brothers."

PHILOKTETES

You who have sent me your longed-for voice   1445
and been revealed to me after a long time,
I will not disobey your authoritative words.

NEOPTOLEMOS

I too cast my judgment in the same way.

HERAKLES

Now don't delay long to act.
The critical moment is here and urges you on,   1450
and the wind for sailing is at the ship's stern.[110]

PHILOKTETES

Come now, let me call upon the land as I set forth.[111]
Farewell, house that kept watch with me,
and Nymphs of the fresh-water meadows,
and deep, masculine pounding of the sea on the cape,   1455
where often my head within the cavern
was struck and sprayed by the south wind;
and Mt. Hermaion often sent
me, in the storms of my sorrow,
a lament in response to my own voice.[112]   1460

---

[109]   The return to anapestic meter signals that the moment of departure and end of the play are at hand.

[110]   *"the critical moment"*: *kairos*. Herakles transforms this term, which elsewhere is associated with the opportunism of Odysseus, Neoptolemos, and the Chorus into a happy occasion for Philoktetes.

[111]   The verb "call upon" is sometimes used of invoking the gods (cf. 736). Philoktetes addresses a prayer to the land, as something divine, in 1464-8.

[112]   *"Mt. Hermaion...my own voice*: Mt. Hermaion ("Hermes' Mountain"), the highest peak in northeastern Lemnos, is mentioned by Klytaimestra in Aischylos, *Agamemnon* 283-85, as a station in her relay of signal fires between Mt. Ida and Mt. Athos in Chalkidike. In *Iliad* 14.229-30, 281-3, Hera stops on Lemnos (though not at Mt. Hermaion) on her journey in the opposite direction. In 1458-60, the echo of Philoktetes' lament from Mt. Hermaion seems consolatory, not "bitter" like the echo described by the Chorus in 188-90.

But now, you springs and Lykian fount,[113]
we're leaving you, we're leaving at last,
though we never entered upon this expectation.
Farewell, you sea-surrounded land of Lemnos:
send me without blame on a fair voyage,   1465
where great Destiny brings me,
and the thoughtful advice of friends, and the all-conquering
divinity who decreed and accomplished these things.[114]

CHORUS
Let us go now all together,
when we have prayed to the Nymphs of the sea   1470
to come as saviors of a return home.[115]

---

[113]   *"Lykian fount"*: presumably a spring sacred to Apollo Lykios. Apollo is
mentioned elsewhere in the play only as the slayer of Achilles (334-36), but
the presence of a spring sacred to him as Apollo Lykios is not surprising,
given the closeness of Lemnos to the region around Troy, where the god
was worshipped by this name. (The epithet *lykios* may refer to Apollo either
as a god of (sun)light who makes everything "white" [*leukainô*] or as a god
associated with wolves [*lykoi*]).

[114]   The *"all-conquering divinity"* is Zeus, whose plans Herakles says he has come
to report. Herakles himself would be numbered among the "friends" by
whose advice Philoktetes is leaving the island.

[115]   *"the Nymphs of the sea"*: the Nereids, the fifty daughters of the sea gods
Nereus and Doris, supposedly had the power to escort voyagers in safety
(cf. *Oidipous at Kolonos* 719). Sappho, in Fragment 5.1-2, calls on them along
with Aphrodite to bring her brother safely back (from Egypt).

Interpretive Essay

THE MYTH

The myth of Philoktetes was well established in Greek poetic tradition long before Sophokles' play was produced in 409 B.C.E.[1] Both the *Iliad* and the *Odyssey* refer to events in the story, as did two epics, no longer extant, in the post-Homeric Epic Cycle: the *Kypria*, which described the background and first nine years of the Trojan War from Zeus' original planning to the situation at the start of the *Iliad*, and the *Little Iliad*, which began with the judgment of the quarrel between Ajax and Odysseus over the arms of the slain Achilles and ended with the Trojans bringing the wooden horse into their city.[2]

---

[1] All dates are B.C.E., unless otherwise indicated. This essay presupposes a reader's familiarity with *Philoktetes* and with the Introduction (above, pp. 1-18).

[2] The Epic Cycle was a series of epics constructed around the *Iliad* and *Odyssey*, filling in the story of the Trojan War and its aftermath. Its contents are preserved in portions of the *Chrêstomatheia*, or *Summary of Useful Knowledge*, by the second-century C.E. grammarian Proklos. These survive mainly in the *Bibliothêkê* (*Library*) of the ninth-century C.E. scholar Photios (Patriarch of Constantinople in 858-67 and 878-86) and partly in some manuscripts of the *Iliad*. The Cycle included the *Kypria*; the *Aithiopis*, which took up where the *Iliad* leaves off and told of the death of Achilles and the dispute over possession of his arms between Odysseus and Ajax, son of Telamon; the *Little Iliad*; the *Sack of Ilion*, on the story of the wooden horse and the fall of Troy, apparently overlapping with the *Little Iliad*; the *Returns*, about the homecomings of various Greek heroes after the war; the *Telegony*, continuing the story of Odysseus from where the *Odyssey* leaves off through his death. The different poems of the Cycle were attributed to various post-Homeric poets but, like the *Iliad* and *Odyssey*, drew for their subject matter on a much older mythological tradition.

The "Catalogue of Ships" in Book 2 of the *Iliad* refers allusively to "Philoktetes skilled with the bow" as

> leader of those who lived around Mêthônê and Thaumakia, and
>   those who
> held Meliboia and rough Olizôn,
> of their seven ships....
> But he lay in the island suffering overwhelming pains,
> in sacred Lemnos, where the sons of the Achaians had left him
> laboring in agony from the evil wound of the malignant water
>   snake;
> there he lay in pain, but soon the Argives beside their ships
> were going to remember King Philoktetes.
>
> (*Il.* 2. 716-25)

According to Proklos, the story was told more fully in the *Kypria* of how Philoktetes was bitten by a snake, when the Greek army stopped at the island of Tenedos on its way to Troy, and then was left behind on Lemnos because of his foul smell. In the *Little Iliad*, also according to Proklos, "Odysseus ambushes and captures the Trojan prince Helenos, and when this man had prophesied about the capture of Troy, Diomedes brings Philoktetes back from Lemnos. And this man, healed by Machaon, kills Paris in single combat." Proklos' wording suggests that Helenos had prophesied that Philoktetes (and his bow?) were needed for the Greeks to take Troy, and therefore Diomedes brought him back to the army.

In Book 3 of the *Odyssey*, Nestor tells Telemachos, "[T]hey say... / ... / that Philoktetes, the glorious son of Poias, came home successfully" after the war (*Od.* 3.188-90). In Book 8, Odysseus, speaking to the Phaeacians, confirms Philoktetes' ability with the bow while boasting of his own skill as an archer:

> I know well how to handle a skillfully made bow;
> I would be the first to shoot and hit my man in a throng
> of enemy warriors, even if very many comrades
> stood nearby and were shooting at the men.
> Only Philoktetes surpassed me with the bow
> in the land of the Trojans, when we Achaians used to shoot with
>   bows.
> But I claim that I am far more skillful than the others,
> as many bread-eating mortals as there now are on the earth.
>
> (*Od.* 8. 215-22)

None of the surviving epic sources tells precisely why Philoktetes was attacked by the snake or how Diomedes brought him from Lemnos to Troy—by persuasion, by force, or in some other way.[3] In Sophokles' play, which sets the scene of the snakebite on the island of Chrysê, at the shrine of its eponymous nymph,[4] Neoptolemos tells Philoktetes that he was bitten because he "approached the guardian of Chrysê, the hidden, / indwelling serpent that guards the roofless shrine" (1327-28). Some later sources, however, specify that Philoktetes was guiding the Greek army to Troy, where as a youth he had accompanied Herakles on an earlier expedition that ended in the sack of the city, and that as he was showing them the shrine of Chrysê, so they might pray for success, he was bitten by the serpent (or, in another version of the story, was wounded when he dropped one of Herakles' poisoned arrows on his own foot).[5]

In the fifth century Philoktetes was mentioned in lyric poetry by Pindar and Bacchylides. In Pindar's first Pythian ode (*Pythian 1.*50-55), Philoktetes serves as a mythological parallel to Hieron, the tyrant of Syracuse who won both athletic and military victories despite a serious illness. An ancient commentator on this passage refers to a poem by Pindar's contemporary, Bacchylides, in which the Greeks brought Philoktetes back to Troy, because "Helenos had prophesied that Troy would not fall without the bow of Herakles."

Philoktetes was the subject of at least a half-dozen Attic tragedies, including plays by Aischylos, Sophokles, and Euripides. In addition to the play we call *Philoktetes*, which in antiquity may have been known as

---

[3]   For what it is worth, Quintus of Smyrna, an epic poet of the fourth or fifth century C.E., suggests in Book 9 of his *Posthomerica* that there was no significant difficulty for the Greeks who "quickly and laughingly brought [Philoktetes] along with his arrows / to their ship on the deep-resounding shore" (*Posthomerica* 9.426-27).

[4]   Chrysê was a small island near Lemnos, which, according to Pausanias, *Description of Greece* 8.33.4, had sunk beneath the sea by the time he was writing in the second century C.E.

[5]   Cf. M. Pipeli, "Philoktetes," *Lexicon Iconigraphicum Mythologiae Classicae* 7.1 (1994), p. 376. A number of later writers, including Pseudo-Aristotle, *On Marvelous Things Heard* 107 (840a17-26), and the first-century B.C.E.-first century C.E. geographer Strabo, *Geographia* 6.254, relate that Philoktetes traveled to Italy after the Trojan War, where he founded several cities, built a temple to Apollo in Makalla (a town near Croton on the Neaethus River, in the foot of the peninsula), and dedicated his bow to the god. He later died fighting in a local war, was buried in Makalla (or, according to another account, near Sybaris), and was worshiped in a hero-cult at the site of his grave. Cf. Pipeli, p. 377.

Philoktetes on Lemnos, Sophokles composed *Philoktetes at Troy*. Besides the Philoktetes-plays of Aischylos, Sophokles, and Euripides, others are attributed to Sophokles' contemporary, Achaios of Eretria; to the poet Antiphon who is known to have been writing around 400; and to Aischylos' nephew, Philokles.

The Philoktetes-plays of Aischylos and Euripides are known mainly from a few extant fragments and from the fifty-second *Discourse* by the Greek orator and popular philosopher Dio Chrysostom (*c.* 40/50-*post* 110 C.E.), in which he compares these two works and Sophokles *Philoktetes*.[6] These three plays have the same general background and setting. The Greek army, which had abandoned Philoktetes on Lemnos on its way to Troy, has learned nine years later from the prophecy of Helenos that his bow and presence are required, if they are to win the war; Odysseus comes (alone in Aischylos, together with Diomedes in Euripides' version of the story) to fetch Philoktetes. In both Aischylos' and Euripides' plays, however, Lemnos is not completely uninhabited as it is in Sophokles' drama; the chorus of each play consists of Lemnians who (however improbably) are visiting Philoktetes for the first time. Aischylos' chorus offer no explanation of their previous neglect, while Euripides' chorus try to excuse their previous absence—implausibly, according to Dio.

In Aischylos' play, Odysseus is not recognized by Philoktetes, gains his trust by a lying story that Agamemnon and Odysseus are dead and Odysseus shamefully disgraced, then somehow manages to get hold of the bow, perhaps during an outbreak of Philoktetes' disease. Subsequently he persuades or compels Philoktetes to accompany him to Troy. Euripides' *Philoktetes* begins with Odysseus explaining to the audience why he and Diomedes have come to Lemnos for Philoktetes and his bow. Athene either has already disguised Odysseus or soon disguises him (as, for example, in *Odyssey* 13.429-38), so that Philoktetes cannot recognize him. When Philoktetes approaches, Odysseus wins his sympathy by claiming to be a refugee and friend of Palamedes, whose death Odysseus had unjustly contrived, and Philoktetes invites him to share his wretched existence. Philoktetes has a Lemnian friend, Aktor, who brings him food

---

[6]   See the Appendix, pp. 119-122, for a translation of this *Discourse*. In *Discourse 59* Dio summarizes the Prologue of Euripides *Philoktetes*. See the English translation by H.L. Crosby in *Dio Chrysostom, Discourses*, Vol. 4, Loeb Classical Library (Cambridge, MA and London, 1946), pp. 440-59. There also are papyrus fragments of ancient "hypotheses" (plot summaries) of both Aischylos' and Euripides' Philoktetes-plays, which were first published in 1952 and 1962, respectively. Euripides' *Philoktetes* was produced in 431, in the same tetralogy as *Medea*; Aischylos' play probably dates from early in the fifth century.

and perhaps news of the arrival of a Trojan embassy, which has come to offer Philoktetes wealth and power if he will help them in the war. The disguised Odysseus and these Trojans have a formal debate; in which Odysseus prevails, perhaps by appealing to Philoktetes' "patriotic" feelings as a Greek. At one point, probably just after a choral ode, Philoktetes suffers a paroxysm; that is when Diomedes enters and steals the bow. Then Odysseus, according to the fragmentary plot summary, "compels" Philoktetes to accompany him to the ship.

SOPHOKLES' PLAY

Sophokles' main mythological and dramatic innovations are evident even from these brief summaries of the Aischylean and Euripidean dramas. First of all, Lemnos is completely "uninhabited, and no mortal sets foot on it" (2). Therefore the Chorus cannot consist of Lemnians, even from another part of the island. Instead, it is comprised of sailors loyal to Neoptolemos, the son of Achilles, who, in a second major departure from the traditional myth, assists Odysseus in the intrigue against Philoktetes. In their entry-song, the Chorus refer to Neoptolemos as "master" (136) and address him as the "man who rule[s] as king / with Zeus' divine scepter" (139-40), but they also call him "child" (141), which suggests that they are significantly older, perhaps veterans who formerly fought under the command of Achilles. Sophokles' third main innovation is to introduce Herakles as the *deus ex machina* who in the end overcomes Philoktetes' intransigence and leads him, against all expectations, to leave the island and rejoin the Greek army at Troy.

That Lemnos is uninhabited must have been surprising, even shocking, to Sophokles' original audience, which would have known that the island for about a hundred years had been (and still was) an Athenian ally and that it had always been populated. The audience also would have been familiar not only with the Aischylean and Euripidean versions of the Philoktetes story in which the island was inhabited, but with other well-known myths involving native Lemnians, which had been represented in both epic and tragedy.[7] By making the island uninhab-

---

7   For example, in *Iliad* 1.593-4, Hephaistos describes how once, when Zeus hurled him from heaven, he "fell in Lemnos..., / where the Sintian men took care of me, after I had fallen." (The *Sinties* seem to have been the aboriginal inhabitants of the island.) Elsewhere in the poem, Eunêos, the son of Jason, is King of Lemnos and sends wine to Agamemnon and Menelaos (7.467-71). He also is said to have once given Patroklos a beautiful mixing bowl as a ransom for Lykaôn, the son of Priam, who had been captured by Achilles (23.746-7). In Aischylos' *Libation Bearers* 631-6, the Chorus sing: "Of evils, the Lemnian takes pride of place / in story, and is lamented as

ited, Sophokles intensifies Philoktetes' isolation and suffering, which are physically, mentally, and socially even more extreme than the isolation and suffering of Sophoklean heroes generally.

THE CHORUS

In formal terms, the Chorus' role as "one of the actors" is reflected by their singing only one fully developed song (676-729). The entry-song (*parodos*) consists of a dialogue between the Chorus (singing in lyric meter) and Neoptolemos (chanting in anapests) that helps to characterize each and that emphasizes the isolation and suffering of Philoktetes. Lines 391-402 correspond metrically with 507-18, but the separation of *strophê* and *antistrophê* by more than one hundred lines makes them less a coherent song than mere lyrical outbursts, in which the Chorus' involvement in the deception of Philoktetes is particularly flagrant and shocking. Later in the play there are two *kommoi* in place of choral songs at 827-64 and 1081-1217.[8] The first of these is another dialogue between the Chorus and Neoptolemos over the sleeping Philoktetes; in the second, Philoktetes and the Chorus join in lamentation, though there also is dramatic give and take as they urge him to accompany them to Troy for his own good and try to justify themselves and Odysseus against his accusations. In these two *kommoi* the Chorus fluctuate in their support of Neoptolemos' intrigue, sympathy for Philoktetes, and impatience with the latter's intransigence. Neither *kommos* does much to situate the events of the drama in a larger intellectual or spiritual framework, and the unusual "free-verse" dialogue in 1169-1217, without the metrically corresponding strophês and antistrophês typical of choral song, works against any sense of choral commentary or clarification of the play's dramatic action.

Throughout the play the Chorus are an integral part of the plot against Philoktetes. From their first words, when they make clear that they are willing to conceal or speak out against the "suspicious man" (136), to "serve" Neoptolemos where necessary (142-43), and to "watch out for the moment that is especially critical for [him]" (151), they are associated with Odysseus' sophistic diction and values and his deceitful

---

abhorrent/ by the people, and one compares / the terrible deed anew to Lemnian disasters. / Through the pollution which the gods hate / the race has perished in dishonor." "The Lemnian evil" refers to the murder by the Lemnian women of all the men in the island (except for Thoas, who was spared by his daughter Hypsipylê). The story must have been so well known to Aischylos' audience that he could make the Chorus refer to it allusively.

[8]   A *kommos* is a song, usually a dirge or lament, sung alternatively by one or more characters and the chorus.

intrigue. When they invoke "all-nourishing mountain-goddess Earth" in timely support of Neoptolemos' false story of how he was robbed of his father's arms (391-402), their "betrayal of all that is inviolable in human life does not hesitate to take cover under the religion of inviolability."[9] In 507-18, they glibly obey Neoptolemos' earlier instructions by seeming to beg him to take pity on Philoktetes. Their concluding wish to bring him home, "escaping / the righteous anger of the gods" (517-18), is exactly parallel in its opportunistic exploitation of religion to their calling on Earth in 391-402. Since neither passage seems to provoke divine punishment, both raise questions about the gods' morality and their relation to human actions—questions that surface elsewhere in the play in the prophecy of Helenos that provides the rationale for Odysseus' intrigue; in Neoptolemos' insistence that Philoktetes accompany them to Troy; in Philoktetes' rhetorical question at 450-52, "How / should I understand these things, how praise them, when / praising the actions of the gods, I find the gods evil?"; in Odysseus' insistence in 993 that by his actions he "[makes the gods] true"; and of course in Herakles' statement that he speaks for Zeus (1415) and his injunction to Philoktetes and Neoptolemos that they "be pious in things having to do with the gods" when they sack Troy, since "father Zeus considers everything else secondary" (1440-42).

At 837-38, the Chorus recommend, in characteristically Odyssean language, that Neoptolemos steal Philoktetes' bow and leave, while he is sleeping off his paroxysm. Even after Neoptolemos rejects this advice on the grounds that Philoktetes himself must come to Troy and comments, "It's an infamous shame to boast with falsehoods of things unaccomplished" (842), they casually remark, "...a god will see to this" (843) and persist in urging him to act "secretly" (850). Later, in the second *kommos*, while trying to persuade Philoktetes to come with them to Troy, they actually defend Odysseus' deception, in Odysseus' own terms, as simply the duty of a representative of Agamemnon and the army: "That man, but one out of many, / at this man's command, / accomplished a public benefit for his friends" (1143-45). The Chorus are neither uncomprehending nor unsympathetic to Philoktetes: even before meeting him they pity his plight (169-90), and the solidarity they express in the second *kommos* is genuine. Nevertheless, they are "sympathetic realists" whose "combination of weak pity and strong self-interest" is predominant,[10] and they are perfectly capable of blaming the victim for his own misfortune:

---

9   K. Reinhardt, *Sophokles*, tr. H. and D. Harvey (Oxford, 1979), p. 171

10   R.P. Winnington Ingram, *Sophocles: An Interpretation* (Cambridge, 1980), pp. 293, 294 n. 44.

> It was you, heavy-doomed man, you who brought it about;
> this fortune does not come from elsewhere, from something
>   greater.
> When it was possible for you to think rationally,
> you chose to embrace the worse, not the better destiny.
> (1095-1100)

Philoktetes replies, "The unlooked-for, concealing/words of a treacherous mind deceived me" (1111-12), to which the Chorus respond complacently, "The gods' doom did this to you, not treachery / by my hand." They then tell him to "...aim your hateful, / ill-fated curse at others. / I want you not to reject my friendship" (1116-22). The impudence of these words is breathtaking, but they need not mean that the Chorus are hypocritical either in their "friendship" or in their attribution of Philoktetes' doom to the gods; Neoptolemos had precisely the same thought (191-200). The difference is that his view changes several times in the course of the play, while theirs remains constant and "by not varying provides, as it were, an axis against which we can plot the movements of their captain's emotions."[11] In effect they remain Odysseus' men to the end, despite their loyalty to Neoptolemos: they make destiny and the gods responsible for what they themselves would do to Philoktetes, just as Odysseus claims to be a servant of Zeus (989-90), and like him they frequently appeal to an impersonal necessity to justify their deception.

The Chorus' participation in Odysseus' intrigue against Philoktetes and their exclusion from the human and divine solidarities with which the play ends are striking. Unlike other Sophoklean choruses, they never rise to a higher intellectual, speculative, or spiritual level, nor do they provide a "choral" voice with which the audience can associate themselves or make a point of departure for their own thoughts. Rather, insofar as the audience might "identify" with the Chorus (as one communal collectivity with another), they too participate in the intrigue. It is characteristic of *Philoktetes* that it is impossible to be sure what the "truth" is or even if there is any "truth" in the various mythological stories that the characters allude to or tell. In another play the Chorus might clarify or interpret such ambiguities. Here, however, their role as "one of the actors," in the manner considered Sophoklean (as opposed to Euripidean) by Aristotle, *Poetics* 18,1456a25-27, leaves things unclear and contributes to the play's distinctive atmosphere of opportunism

---

[11]   Ibid., p. 294 n. 44.

and its problematic lack of any consolatory, enlightening, or uplifting perspective on its own events and values.

NEOPTOLEMOS

As far as is known, Neoptolemos was not directly associated with Philoktetes in traditional mythology prior to Sophokles' play, except that both were necessary for the sack of Troy.[12] Nor is there an earlier connection between Neoptolemos and Odysseus, apart from an obscure reference in Proklos' summary of the *Returns* to a meeting between the two in Marôneia (in Thrace), shortly after the end of the Trojan War.[13] By introducing Neoptolemos into the story of the retrieval of Philoktetes from Lemnos, Sophokles gives his play remarkable dramatic and moral complexity through a contrast between innocence and experience in the realm of politics and a critique of traditional conceptions of nobility and heroism that seem to go beyond anything that might have transpired in the Philoktetes-plays of Aischylos and Euripides.

Neoptolemos is the son of Achilles and self-proclaimed heir to his inborn, "natural" integrity (88-89), but Odysseus easily plays on the youth's desire for the kind of heroic glory associated with his father— the glory that would come from the supreme achievement of sacking Troy—in order to seduce him into using distinctively non-Achillean, typically Odyssean lies and treachery to "deceive Philoktetes' mind with your words" (55), to "be the thief of the invincible weapons" (78) that will make the capture of the city possible. Although Neoptolemos initially finds such lying and deception "shameful" (108), he agrees for the sake of his own "profit" (112) to "put aside all shame and do it" (120). His self-professed natural reluctance to act "by evil contrivance" (88) and preference "to take the man by force / instead of deceit" (90-91), and "to fail / by doing well rather than to conquer by evil means" (94-95), are no match for Odysseus' paternal reassurance that speech rather than action is what prevails in life (96-99) and his deft assertion that he does not consider it shameful to lie "if the lie brings salvation" (109).

---

[12] According to Proklos' summary of the *Little Iliad*, after "Diomedes brings back Philoktetes from Lemnos," and he is healed by Machaon and kills Paris in single combat, "Odysseus brings Neoptolemos from Skyros and gives him his father's arms."

[13] "Neoptolemos on the advice of Thetis makes his journey [from Troy] on foot; when he is in Thrace, he overtakes Odysseus in Maroneia." This meeting is mentioned nowhere else in extant Greek literature. (In *Odyssey* 9.196-200, Odysseus tells the Phaeacians that Maron, a Thracian priest of Apollo, gave him "a strong, dark wine" in return for Odysseus saving him and his family during the sack of Ismaros.)

Neoptolemos turns out to be a consummate liar: in a clever story that resembles, in its mixture of truth and falsehood, the lying tales told by Odysseus in the second half of the *Odyssey*, Neoptolemos depicts his own purported mistreatment at the hands of Odysseus and the sons of Atreus as closely analogous to that of Philoktetes himself. In this way he succeeds in gaining Philoktetes' friendship and trust, which he later betrays in order to get possession of the bow, after Philoktetes entrusts it to him for safekeeping. It turns out that the relationship of friendship and reciprocal solidarity so movingly established by Neoptolemos and Philoktetes (667-73) is itself a component of Neoptolemos' treachery. Moreover, insofar as this relationship is partly based on Philoktetes' old friendship with Achilles (242), Neoptolemos' betrayal of Philoktetes is also, in a fundamental way, a betrayal of his own father and of the nobility he claimed to inherit (88-89), as well as of the father-son relationship that has come to exist between Philoktetes and himself.[14]

Neoptolemos is so affected by the sight of Philoktetes' paroxysm that he confesses his treachery (912-16). Nevertheless, the compassion he feels at the sight of Philoktetes' physical suffering and the moral quandary occasioned by the sense that he has betrayed his "own nature" (895, 897, 902-903, 906) do not, at first, prevent him from holding on to the bow and justifying himself to Philoktetes on the grounds that "a great necessity / compels these things" (921-22). Neoptolemos may realize that he cannot simply abandon the sleeping Philoktetes, as Odysseus had done nine years earlier (271-75); that it is not enough simply to have gotten possession of the bow and arrows, which was Odysseus' and his own goal in the Prologue (78, 113). Nevertheless, his conviction "that we have hunted / down this bow in vain, if we sail without him. / The crown is his; he's the one the god said to bring" (839-41), suggests that he still sees nothing wrong with forcing Philoktetes against his will to participate in the war for the sake of the Greek army and of Neoptolemos' own prospective glory. Despite his bond of friendship with the son of Poias (671-73), Neoptolemos continues implicitly to endorse Odysseus' instrumental treatment of Philoktetes as a mere means to an end—"the possession of victory" (81, cf. 1052). He still speaks the typically Odyssean language of impersonal necessity ("must," 921-22-54, 77, 982, 993-94), whether strategically, to persuade Philoktetes, or in order to veil from himself the true reason why Philoktetes must come to Troy. In 841 Neoptolemos complacently and self-servingly assumes that "the god" is on his side, just as earlier in the play he told the Chorus that Philoktetes'

---

[14]   Philoktetes calls Neoptolemos "my son" or "my child" fifty-two times in the play; in effect he wins a kind of contest with Odysseus to see whose "son" the son of Achilles really is.

"sufferings, if I have any understanding, / are divine" (192-93) and that "there's no way the gods are not concerned / lest this man draw against Troy too soon / the unopposable shafts of the gods, / until the time comes in which it is said / that the city must be conquered by them" (196-200). Neoptolemos continues to make this assumption even after returning the bow, when he tells Philoktetes that his wound and sickness are a stroke of "divine fortune" (1326) and invokes the prophecy of "Helenos, the best of seers" (1338) as a reason why Philoktetes should "give your agreement willingly" to go to Troy, be healed, and win the "highest glory" (1343-47).

Neoptolemos returns the bow and arrows to Philoktetes, after telling Odysseus that he is going "to undo the mistake I made earlier" / ... / "the one I made by obeying you and the whole army—" / ... / "taking a man by treachery and shameful deception" (1224, 1226, 1228); that he will return what "I've taken...shamefully and unjustly" (1234), and "try to retrieve / the shameful mistake I committed" (1248-49). After Philoktetes regains his weapons, he praises Neoptolemos in the terms that mean the most to him:

> You've shown your nature, my child, the stock
> from which you were born—not from Sisyphos as a father
> but from Achilles who, when he was alive,
> had the greatest glory, as he now does among the dead.[15]
> (1310-13)

Nevertheless, even though Neoptolemos manages to escape Odysseus' hold on him and earn Philoktetes' praise, the stability and significance of his return to "the Achillean standard" and his ethical disposition remain ambiguous and problematic.[16] For example, there is a clear allusion, in Herakles' warning to remain pious during the sack of Troy (1440-44), to Neoptolemos' notorious impiety on that occasion, when he slaughtered Priam on the altar of Zeus. Furthermore, because Neoptolemos' pity and respect for Philoktetes seem, on the surface, so similar to Achilles' for Priam in Book 24 of the *Iliad*, the reminder of the son's ruthless impiety toward the helpless king during the sack of the city is all the more troubling. So too is Neoptolemos' exaggerated statement to Philoktetes that "it's not right for anyone / either to pity or to pardon" those "who cling to self-inflicted harm, / as you do..."

---

[15]   On "Sisyphos as a father," lines 384, 417, and 625 with notes.

[16]   I borrow the phrase "the Achillean standard" from B.M.W. Knox, *The Heroic Temper: Studies in Sophoclean Tragedy* (Berkeley and Los Angeles, 1964), p. 123.

(1318-20). This is by no means an Achillean sentiment, and if an audience or reader were to recall the unflattering story of Neoptolemos' eventual death at Delphi at the hands of Orestes (as told, for example, in Euripides' *Andromache*), the instability of his return to the Achillean standard would be still more evident.

Near the end of the play, Herakles speaks of Neoptolemos and Philoktetes as guarding one another at Troy "like two lions pasturing together" (1436-37.) This apparently positive simile, however, recalls *Iliad* 10.297, where Odysseus and Diomedes go "like two lions through the dark night" on the spying expedition during which they capture, deceive, and butcher the Trojan spy Dolon, then proceed to slaughter the sleeping Thracian king, Rhesos, and his men and steal his horses. Thus, even in a passage that is supposed to present Neoptolemos in a favorable light, he does not entirely escape an association with the ethically ambiguous and unsavory Odysseus. The hint a few lines later of Neoptolemos' impious behavior during the sack of Troy reinforces the allusion in 1436-37 to the scene in Book 10 of the *Iliad* where Odysseus and Diomedes act more opportunistically and less honorably than anywhere else in that epic. It is worth remembering, too, that in Euripides' *Philoktetes*, Diomedes joined Odysseus in the successful intrigue against Philoktetes. Thus, through the lion simile, with its distinctive use of the dual, the figurative association of Neoptolemos with the heroes of *Iliad* 10 also aligns him with the deceivers of Philoktetes in that earlier play.

This complex intertextuality opens up confusing problems of interpretation just as the action of the play seems to be shutting them down as part of its "happy" ending. As an audience or readers realize that they know more about Neoptolemos than first meets the eye, they are drawn into a critical perspective that brings with it feelings of regret and loss. Presumably no one in the audience wants to give up the identification with Neoptolemos that has been carefully cultivated by the play's story of his apparently successful moral education into his inherent nobility. Yet the knowledge that something in his character and destiny is warped and can't be straightened, undercuts this identification and with it the values for which he seems to stand.

Odysseus

Odysseus seems to be completely excluded from the play's ending: he exits shortly after his empty threat to "convey" Philoktetes to Troy "by force, / whether or not the son of Achilles is willing" (1297-98), never reappears on stage, and is not even mentioned by Herakles in the final scene. Nevertheless, from one point of view, when Philoktetes agrees to join the army and help bring about the sack of Troy, Odysseus gets what he wanted all along, even though he appeared to be defeated; and getting what he wanted may be enough for one whose stated ambition is "victory in all things" (1052). Furthermore, though Herakles declares (as Odysseus had done earlier) that only Philoktetes and Neoptolemos together "have the strength to take the plain of Troy" (1434-5; cf. 115), the audience or reader would remember that in the *Odyssey* and the mythological tradition generally, the chief credit for capturing the city belonged to Odysseus, the "sacker of cities" *par excellence*. Herakles' epiphany and his authoritative words about Zeus' plans for Philoktetes do not completely efface Odysseus' opportunistic success.

More than any other character in *Philoktetes*, Odysseus brings into the play the political and moral world of late fifth-century Athens, as it is described and represented in Thucydides' *The Peloponnesian War*. For example, his emphasis on lying as the only way in which Neoptolemos can get possession of Philoktetes' weapons and gain his assistance in the larger political goal of winning the Trojan War, recalls Diodotos' statement in Thucydides' Mytilenean Debate that lies are a normal feature of political discourse—"that it is equally necessary that the man arguing for the most terrible proposals win over the people by deceit and the man with better advice make himself trusted by lying." [17] From this position (which is Odysseus' position) of straightforward *Real-Politik*, Neoptolemos' hesitation in the Prologue to tell lies and to deceive Philoktetes makes him seem exceptionally innocent (*euêthês*, "of good character," "naïve," "simple," to use the Thucydidean term).

In fact, Thucydides comments that among the changes in the social and moral fabric brought about by the revolutions and civil conflicts that arose throughout Greece during the Peloponnesian War, "the simplicity (*to euêthes*) that is especially found in noble natures disappeared because it became ridiculous" (3.83.1). In the world he describes, "nature" is not a matter of inherent innocence or nobility, as Neoptolemos seems to believe when he uses these terms (e.g. 88-89), but of an inborn disposition toward brutality and exploitation, grounded in an appetite for victory that stems, in turn, from acquisitiveness and personal ambition (3.82.8). This is a world in which Sophokles' Odysseus would be immediately at home. It is no accident that Odysseus' uses the word "noble" (*gennaios*), a term that suggests naturally inherited excellence, both seductively at 50, to convince Neoptolemos to "be of service" in "deceiv[ing] Philoktetes' mind with your words" (53, 55), and sarcastically at 1068, to stop him from feeling too much sympathy for Philoktetes after stealing his bow,

---

17   Quotations from Thucydides are taken from *Thucydides, The Peloponnesian War*, translated, with Introduction and Notes, by Steven Lattimore (Indianapolis and Cambridge, 1998).

"so you won't ruin our good fortune" (1069).

One main feature of Odysseus' rhetorical style, which he shares with many speakers in Thucydides, is the tendency to understand, explain, or justify his own and others' actions and desires by invoking some impersonal, external, supposedly objective necessity, such as divine inevitability. It is not always easy to know when an argument that something happened or must happen in a certain way because of necessity is meant as a genuine explanation of reality, a rhetorical ploy to persuade others to do as one wishes, or an effort to evade responsibility for one's actions. In any case, such arguments, involving language and syntax associated with compulsion or necessity, are common in the speech of Odysseus (e.g. 50-57, 993-94) and of Neoptolemos when he is acting as Odysseus' agent (e.g. 116, 915, 921-22). They are one feature of the representation of Odysseus (and, for part of the play, Neoptolemos) as a particular kind of political figure, with a distinctive rhetorical and ethical style recognizable from contemporary Athens and from the pages of Thucydides.

Another feature of Odysseus' rhetorical style, related to his political role as representative of the Greek army at Troy, is his frequent association with the language of violence. In the roughly contemporaneous plays of Euripides produced during "the last years of the Peloponnesian War," Odysseus is regularly represented or referred to "as a type of the new political extremists, who armed with Sophistic rhetoric, dominated the Athenian assembly with their ferocious policies of repression and aggrandizement."[18] Odysseus is referred to three times in the play, by a kind of naming periphrasis familiar from Homeric epic, as "the violence (*bia*) of Odysseus": by Philoktetes in 314, by Neoptolemos echoing him in 321, and by the false Merchant, whom Odysseus himself ventriloquates, in 592. This circumlocution, however, is never used in the *Iliad* or *Odyssey* of Odysseus himself, which makes it all the more striking that he should be named in this way in *Philoktetes*. No other character in the play is spoken of by such a periphrasis, and there is only one other example in extant Sophoklean drama ("the violence of Iphitos," *The Women of Trachis*, 38). Thus physical and verbal violence of the kind directed against Philoktetes is distinctively characteristic of Odysseus, and this is reflected in the way he is spoken of by himself and others.

The association of violence with Odysseus might seem surprising, since in the Homeric epics Odysseus is the figure *par excellence* of mentality (*noos*) and cunning intelligence (*mêtis*), with a penchant for treacher-

---

[18]   Knox, *The Heroic Temper*, p. 124 with p. 186 n. 15.

ous deception (*dolos*). As such, he is frequently opposed to heroes of outstanding physical strength and prowess, notably Achilles and Ajax, as well as to figures of brute force, such as Polyphemos. In *Philoktetes*, Odysseus is, of course, still a figure of cunning intelligence and treacherous deception, but these mental qualities are represented as manifestations, sources, and techniques of violence rather than as contrasting features of character and disposition. Perhaps this fundamental change in the characterization of Odysseus is a function of the parallel between the ongoing Trojan War in the play and the Peloponnesian War, which in 409 had lasted more than two decades. Both Neoptolemos, in his false persona (563), and Philoktetes (945, 985) speak indignantly of the Greeks' intention to "bring them by force" (*ek bias agein*) to participate in the war, an idiom that occurs nowhere else in extant Sophoklean drama and that seems to be associated specifically with the war effort.[19]

Odysseus actually becomes physically more violent in the course of the play. At the beginning, when Neoptolemos is reluctant to lie but willing to bring Philoktetes by direct violence (*bia*, 90,92), Odysseus realizes that this approach will not work (103). Later, however, when Neoptolemos confesses the truth to Philoktetes, and Philoktetes threatens to kill himself rather than go to Troy, Odysseus tells his men, "Seize him! Don't let him do this!" (1003) At 1254-55, Odysseus actually reaches for his sword, before backing away from fighting Neoptolemos. He later threatens to "convey" Philoktetes "to the plain of Troy by force (*bia*) / whether or not the son of Achilles is willing" (1297-98), only to flee when Philoktetes aims an arrow at him.

Such intra-communal violence was a fundamental feature of Greek political reality in the late fifth century. It arose in Athens with particular savagery during the civil strife and revolutions of 411-410, just a year or two before the production of *Philoktetes*. Commentators on the play have recognized since antiquity that Odysseus resembles contemporary Athenian popular leaders, especially in his readiness to use both physical and rhetorical violence to further his personal and political ends.[20] He nowhere seems more Athenian than in the final lines of the Prologue, when he tells the now acquiescent Neoptolemos (133-34),

---

19 Cf. Thucydides' famous description of war as "a violent teacher and teacher of violence" (*biaios didaskalos*, 3.82.2, my translation)

20 Apropos of Odysseus' assertion in 99 "that it's speech, not action, that leads the way in all things", an ancient commentator says, "The poet slanders the political leaders of his own time as succeeding in all things through speech."

> May Hermes the Escort, the Trickster, guide us both,
> and Victory Athena the City-Goddess, who always saves me.

Here Odysseus anachronistically and tellingly endows Athena, his traditional protectress in the Homeric epics, with cult titles that would have been immediately recognizable to a late fifth-century Athenian audience as referring to their own civic religion. Victory Athena (*Athêna Nikê*) was the personification of triumphant Athenian imperialism. She was worshiped in the small temple of Nikê located near the southwest corner of the acropolis, just south of the Propylaea or entrance to the complex. Athena the City-Goddess (*Athêna Polias*) was worshipped in an older cult as the protectress of the acropolis, the city of Athens, and Attica generally. She was represented by an old olive-wood statue housed in the Erechtheum, the temple on the north side of the acropolis that was still under construction in 409. The effect of Odysseus' invocation of "Victory Athena the City-Goddess" is to associate his own rhetoric, values, and desire for victory everywhere and by any means with the political rhetoric, values and actions of contemporary Athens.[21]

Another striking feature of Odysseus' rhetorical style is his conspicuous use of language associated with political and moral values characteristic of the fifth-century Sophistic movement—values that stand in radical contrast to traditional conceptions of heroic nobility, nature, and honor.[22] At 77-80 he tells Neoptolemos,

---

[21]   There is one other noteworthy connection between the victimization of Philoktetes and the civic religion of contemporary Athens, though it has no relation to Odysseus. At 1326-28, Neoptolemos tells Philoktetes, "You're sick with this pain by divine fortune, / since you approached the guardian of Chrysê, the hidden, / indwelling serpent that guards the roofless shrine." "Indwelling serpent" (*oikourôn ophis*, 1328) is a technical term for the sacred serpent living in the Erechtheum, which represented the quasi-historical King Erichthonios and guarded the temple. (Cf. Aristophanes, *Lysistrata* 759, Herodotos 8.41, Pausanias I.24.7). The association of Athenian civic religion with the attack on Philoktetes here and in 134 almost makes it seem, anachronistically, that he is a victim of Athens itself.

[22]   On Odysseus and the sophists in connection with Sophokles' *Philoktetes*, see N. Worman, "Odysseus *Panourgos*: The Liar's Style in Tragedy and Oratory," *Helios* 26 (1999), pp. 35-68; *The Cast of Character: Style in Greek Literature* (Austin, 2002), pp. 139-48. Cf. M.W. Blundell, "The Moral Character of Odysseus in *Philoctetes*," *Greek, Roman and Byzantine Studies* 28 (1987), pp. 307-29. P.W. Rose, "Sophokles' *Philoktetes* and the Teachings of the Sophists: A Counteroffensive," in *Sons of the Gods, Children of the Earth: Ideology and Literary Form in Ancient Greece* (Ithaca and London, 1992), pp. 266-330, studies the conflict between traditional and Sophistic values in the play.

No, this is just the thing in which you must be clever, so you
may become the thief of the invincible weapons.
I know well, my son, that by nature you were not born
to contrive such things or utter such evils.

"To be clever" (*sophisthênai*, 77) and "to contrive" (*technasthai*, 80) are
activities that imply learning and knowing how to use an acquired craft
or technique, as opposed to acting naturally. This sort of technique and
know-how were taught by the Sophists to their students and typically
applied to solving specific problems or achieving particular social and
political goals, unlike such qualities as nobility or honor that, in the traditional conception, would always dictate the same behavior, regardless
of the specific occasion or circumstances.

It is no accident that Odysseus, just after describing how he had
marooned Philoktetes ten years earlier, tells Neoptolemos (11-14),

But why should I go on speaking
of these things? We have no time for long speeches.
He may learn that I've come, and I'll waste the whole
clever plan by which I expect to catch him right away.

"Clever plan" (*sophisma*), like "to be clever" (77) and "to contrive" (80),
clearly associates Odysseus with the fifth-century Sophistic movement. So does the word "clever" (*sophos*) that is used by Odysseus in
his description of the two prizes Neoptolemos will gain for himself, if
he agrees to "hunt" (116) the bow of Philoktetes by telling lies: "you
would be called both clever and noble (*sophos...agathos*) at the same
time" (119)—a formulation that is particularly striking because it is a
sophistic transformation of the traditional description of an Athenian
gentleman as "fine and noble" (*kalos...agathos*). Similarly, Odysseus tells
Neoptolemos (126-31),

If you seem to me to be
taking too much time, I'll send this same man out again
another time, after disguising his outward appearance
in the character of a merchant ship's captain, so he won't be
    recognized.
From him, my child, as he speaks craftily, receive
what is advantageous in his words, whenever he says
    something.

"What is advantageous" (131) is a Sophistic term that has no fixed meaning but is inherently relativistic, since "what is advantageous" varies in varying circumstances. "What is advantageous" often stands in contrast to "what is just," but sometimes it is provocatively identified with the latter concept, as in the first book of Plato's *Republic*, where the Sophist Thrasymachos defines justice as "that which is advantageous for (or: "in the interest of") the stronger," or in Plato's *Gorgias*, where Kallikles, speaking in the language and style of a Sophist, argues baldly and boldly that "might makes right." Odysseus' language and values would certainly have been recognizable to a late fifth-century audience, and are still recognizable today, as those of an opportunistic Sophist. The power to have his way and to do what will be to his advantage at any given time are all the justification he needs for his words and actions. As he tells Philoktetes (1048-52),

> ...I limit myself to just one word:
> where there's a need for such men, such a man am I;
> and wherever there's a competition of just and good men,
> you would find no one more righteous than I.
> My nature is to desire victory in all things....

"Such men" (literally: "men of such a sort"), like "that which is advantageous," is a relative term with no absolute or consistent meaning; Odysseus' appropriation of the word "nature" cannot conceal how far removed his relativistic values are from the inherited standards of natural nobility and honor that are associated elsewhere in the play with Neoptolemos, his father Achilles, and Philoktetes.[23]

In the Prologue, urging Neoptolemos to deceive Philoktetes, Odysseus says (81-85),

> Since...the possession of victory is something sweet to gain,
> bring yourself to do it; we'll appear to be just on another
>   occasion.
> Give yourself to me now for a short, shameless
> portion of a day, and then for the rest of time
> be called the most pious of all mortals.

---

[23]   See M.W. Blundell, "The *Phusis* of Neoptolemos in Sophocles' *Philoctetes*," *Greek Tragedy*, ed. I. McAuslan and P. Walcot (Oxford, 1993), pp. 104-15.

Odysseus casually defers such basic virtues as justice and righteousness to an indefinite future, where what counts is only a matter of *appearing* "just" and *being called* "most righteous," not integrity and identity in some absolute sense. This relativism is completely at odds with a traditional notion of heroic excellence, according to which there should be no disjunction between how one appears and is spoken of and one's fundamental identity.

Odysseus' goal is to be effective in the moment: he enjoins Neoptolemos to "receive what is advantageous in [the] words" of the false merchant ship's captain, "whenever he says something" (131). This emphasis on the critical moment, which is picked up by both Neoptolemos (466, 1279) and the Chorus (151, 837), is one aspect of Odysseus' distinctive, amoral opportunism and one feature of the Sophistic rhetorical style through which he would have evoked for the play's original audience their contemporary political leaders. Nothing could be further removed from the Achillean nature to which Neoptolemos lays claim or from the genuine nobility and heroism of Odysseus' victim, the much-abused Philoktetes.

PHILOKTETES

If Odysseus is a creature of triumphant opportunism, whose emphasis on "victory in all things" involves seizing the critical moment, Philoktetes is associated with the long passage of time, in which he has suffered as a victim but endured stubbornly in a kind of heroic triumph over his victimization. He undergoes intense, recurrent physical pain from the disease caused by his snakebite, and the outbreak of this disease as he and Neoptolemos prepare to leave the island (730-826) is literally and dramatically at the heart of the play. Odysseus' earlier references to its symptoms (7-11), Neoptolemos' description of rags stained with matter discharged from Philoktetes' ulcerated foot (39), and the Chorus' mention of his "far-off cry" and anguished "lament" (207-9, 216-8) give some idea of Philoktetes' suffering. Nothing, however, is as vivid and affecting as the sheer physical agony that is the main symptom of his paroxysm. This paroxysm leads to the final success of Odysseus' intrigue and Neoptolemos' deception, because it brings Philoktetes to entrust his bow to the son of Achilles. At the same time, however, it gives rise to Neoptolemos' moral awakening, as he comes to pity Philoktetes' divinely inflicted suffering rather than the treating it merely as a means to his own ends of conquering Troy and winning heroic glory.

The psychological pain arising, from Philoktetes' abandonment and isolation on Lemnos, is, in its own way, as intense as his physical agony. Even before meeting him, the Chorus "pity...the way— / with no one of mortals to care for him, / unable to see the face of a comrade— / he is sick ... / and goes mad at every need / that arises" (169-75). Later, Philoktetes tells Neoptolemos that he is "alone, / deserted, so beset by troubles, without a companion or friend" (227-28), that there is "not a man in the place, no one / to assist me, no one who could help me in my suffering / to support my disease" (280-82). In his isolation Philoktetes can speak only to "you harbors, you headlands, you communities of / mountain beasts, you steep rocks... / ...my usual companions" (936-38); he hears only the sound of his own voice, the echo of his own lamentations (188-90). He is so utterly cut off from human contact that he becomes part of the animal ecology of the island: without his bow, as he tells Neoptolemos, "I will die and furnish a feast for those off whom I used to feed, / and those whom I once hunted will now hunt me. / Wretched me, I will pay blood for blood in reprisal..." (957-59).

Philoktetes is "sick with a savage disease" (173) from the "savage / mark of the man-destroying serpent" (266-67); he refers to himself and is referred to by others as "having become savage" (226, 1321), though it remains unclear to what extent he has been made savage through his victimization by others and to what degree he has made himself savage through hatred of his enemies. One measure of Philoktetes' savagery is his physical isolation on the uninhabited island; another is his social isolation, as expressed in the repeated sense that there is no one to befriend and pity him. Yet even after Neoptolemos has earned his friendship and trust by returning the bow, Philoktetes continues to reject his friendly advice (1383-6); he still refuses to sail to Troy and rejoin the army, despite Neoptolemos' assertion that "those who cling to self-inflicted harm, / as you do—it's not right for anyone / either to pity or to pardon them. / You have become savage..." (1318-21). Philoktetes is, as it were, caught in the necessities of his hatred of Odysseus and the sons of Atreus. This intense hatred not only prevails over all attempts at rational persuasion, but constitutes, at least in the eyes of Neoptolemos, a willful, savage rejection of the very pity and human solidarity that Philoktetes had earlier claimed he lacked, because of his abandonment on Lemnos.

In the opening lines of the play, Odysseus tells Neoptolemos,

> This is the shore of Lemnos, a land circled by the sea;
> it's uninhabited, and no mortal sets foot on it.

"Circled by the sea" (*perirhutos*) calls to mind *amphirhutos*, an adjective from the same root and with the same meaning that is used near the beginning of the *Odyssey* to describe Ogygia, the sea-surrounded island of Kalypso on which Odysseus is stranded (1.50; cf. 198). This is one small example of how *Philoktetes* generates meaning through verbal echoes of the *Iliad* and *Odyssey*, echoes which constitute situational and structural allusions to the two epics. Even though Odysseus in the play is Philoktetes' hated enemy, the situation of Philoktetes on Lemnos is patterned after that of Odysseus in the *Odyssey*. The association of these two characters with one another is sometimes suggested by specific details: for example, captivity on an island "surrounded by the sea," or the "two-mouthed cave" in which Philoktetes dwells, which recalls the two-mouthed cave of the Nymphs on Ithaca (*Od.* 13.103-12, esp. 109-11). More fundamentally, however, insofar as he is marooned on an island where he cannot function as his normal self, Philoktetes might be thought of as symbolically dead, like the Homeric Odysseus on the island of Kalypso and in many of the lands to which he travels. Philoktetes even calls himself "a corpse among the living" (1018) and tells Odysseus, "I have long been dead, as far as you're concerned" (1030). The main movement of the play is from symbolic death to heroic rebirth, culminating in a "return home" (*nostos*, 1471)—a movement that recalls Odysseus' repeated escapes from literal or symbolic death and his return home to Ithaca, where he re-establishes his distinctive heroic identity as husband, father, and king.[24]

At the same time, Philoktetes also can be thought of, in Iliadic rather than Odyssean terms, as patterned after Achilles. Despite their physical and psychological isolation, both Achilles and Philoktetes long for friendship and human solidarity. Nevertheless, when confronted by an "embassy" from Agamemnon, led by Odysseus, both figures stubbornly reject the benefits that are offered to induce them to rejoin the Greek army. They refuse to compromise with those by whom they consider themselves dishonored and disrespected, and their integrity cannot be shaken by force or persuasion.

The similarity, however, between the Iliadic Achilles and Philoktetes is complicated, because in the play Neoptolemos, who claims to have the inborn nobility of his father Achilles, allies himself with Odysseus, despite the longstanding tradition in which "the contrasted figures of Odysseus and Achilles had become...mythical and literary prototypes of two entirely different worlds of thought and feeling."[25] Neoptolemos, who befriends, betrays, and again befriends Philoktetes, represents, in contrast to Philoktetes, an ethically compromised, fifth-century tragedic version of the epic Achilles: despite his inborn nobility and eventual

---

[24] Cf. D. Frame, *The Myth of Return in Early Greek Epic* (New Haven and London, 1978), pp. 1-80.

[25] Knox, *The Heroic Temper*, p. 121.

rejection of Odyssean treachery, ultimately, as I have argued (above, pp. 99-100), he falls short of the Achillean heroic standard familiar from the *Iliad*. Odysseus too represents a distinctively fifth-century version of his epic self: for example, while he lies in the *Odyssey* for his own advantage, he does not suborn others to do so as in *Philoktetes*, nor are his falsehoods—for example, his deception of Polyphemos and the six lying tales he tells in the second half of the poem—ethically problematic in the ways they are in the play.

Odysseus' initial description of Lemnos as "uninhabited, and no mortal sets foot on it" (2), implies that he does not consider Philoktetes himself to be truly human. Presumably, Odysseus means to prepare Neoptolemos to hunt him down and steal his bow without sympathy or remorse. It soon transpires, however, that the island on which "no mortal sets foot" (*astipton*) is inhabited precisely by the "footstep" (*stibos*) of Philoktetes. This relatively rare word is used repeatedly and conspicuously in the first third of the play to suggest both Philoktetes' painful way of "planting his footsteps" (29. 48, 157, 163, 206) and the island's paths along which he laboriously struggles. At 162-3, for example, the Choros imagine him "dragging his / footsteps...in need of food," and at 206-9 they link his struggle to crawl with his cry of pain. These and similar passages vividly evoke Philoktetes' physical suffering and give the lie to Odysseus' casual description of the island as "uninhabited, and no mortal sets foot on it." In a sense, however, when Philoktetes later pleads with Neoptolemos to bring him home, he confirms Odysseus' words: "No, don't leave me alone / in such isolation, apart from the tread (*stibon*) of human beings, / but save me..." (486-88). The human companionship implied by the "tread of human beings" would be a particularly meaningful consequence of his deliverance.

Just as Lemnos, on which "no mortal sets foot," turns out to be trodden by the "footstep" of Philoktetes, so the "uninhabited" island contains his "habitation," or dwelling. In Greek the word "home" (*oikos*) usually means a product of human culture, a constructed house occupied by an extended family sharing a domestic cult. By contrast, the two-mouthed cave in which Philoktetes resides (31, 32, 40) is a prominent natural, rather than cultural, feature of the island. Odysseus belittles this dwelling, referring to it in language that suggests a "sheepfold" (19), just as he describes Philoktetes as having "gone out to bring home something to eat" (43) in language that might call to mind a wild animal feeding rather than a human being (cf. 163). Philoktetes, however, to some degree domesticates the cave by "provision...that would make it a home" (32), and Neoptolemos speaks of Philoktetes' "home with doors at both ends, / his rocky bed-chamber" (159-60).

The simultaneously non-human and all-too-human aspects of Philoktetes' habitation are emphasized throughout the play. On the one hand, he tells Neoptolemos and the Chorus, "To dwell with a roof over my head and a fire / provides everything except that I not be diseased" (298-99). On the other hand, the first question he asks Neoptolemos is, "Who in the world are you, who have put in with a sailor's oar / to this land that is uninhabited and without harbors?" (220-21). At different times during the play, Odysseus, Neoptolemos, and Philoktetes all use the word "home" of the native lands that they left behind on the expedition to Troy, often while expressing the desire or intention to return to them (58, 60, 240, 311, 383, 469, 548). The paradoxical nature of Philoktetes' "home" suggests that, although with great effort he remains human, he also has, in a sense, been turned into an animal, a specimen of nature rather than of culture, by his nine years of forced exile from human society.

Lemnos itself is an island of similar ambivalence. Just as it is both inhabited and uninhabited, so it helps to characterize Philoktetes as both sub-human and superhuman. On the one hand, the island reduces him to cries of physical agony (205-9, 213-8) and psychological pain at his isolation in a place with "no anchorage at all," to which "no sailor puts in...willingly" (301-303). Yet it also gives him the opportunity to prove himself a special kind of human being—to maintain his life and his integrity, his loyalty to friends and hatred of his enemies, in the face of unspeakable suffering. Earlier, in his helplessness after Neoptolemos and Odysseus have taken his bow, he sees himself as part of the island and its natural ecology:

> You harbors, you headlands, you communities of
> mountain beasts, you steep rocks—I make
> this lament to you, my usual companions,
> since I know of no one else to whom I might speak.
> ...
> You rock with two entrances, I'll return
> to you again—but naked, without the means to live.
> I'll wither away in this dwelling, alone,
> slaying no winged bird, no mountain beast
> with this bow; rather I myself, in my misery,
> will die and furnish a feast for those off whom I use to feed,
> and those whom I once hunted will now hunt me.
>
> (936-39, 952-58)

Later, however, in the final lines, as he is leaving, Philoktetes warmly addresses the same physical features of the landscape that previously had seemed hostile and oppressive. Where formerly he emphasized the difficulty of obtaining something to drink (292-95), in these final lines he mentions the "springs and Lykian fount" (1461). Earlier he (somewhat disparagingly) referred to the "two-mouthed cave" as "this poor roof" (287) and as his "dwelling that is no dwelling" (534). He also addressed it negatively in 1081-85:

> you hollow of cavernous rock,
> hot and ice cold by turns,
> so I wasn't, after all, ever going
> to leave you, wretched me, but you
> will be my witness, even as I am dying.

Now, however, Philoktetes speaks of "the house that kept watch with me" (1453), using a word for "house" (*melathron*) that originally meant "roofbeam" and that clearly suggests a constructed product of human craft and culture rather than a natural cave, implying the house's human solidarity with him by describing it as sharing in his "ke[eping] watch." Similarly, Philoktetes recalls how "Mt. Hermaion often sent / me, in the storms of my sorrow, / a lament in response to my own voice" (1458-60), though earlier, at least according to the Chorus, Philoktetes heard only the "babbling Echo" of his bitter complaints (188-90) and had "no one in the land as a neighbor to his troubles, / beside whom he could bewail the disease / with groans that called forth a response…" (692-94).

As he is leaving, Philoktetes can even feel the island as populated by "Nymphs of the fresh-water meadows," whose femininity is complemented by the beneficent "deep masculine pounding of the sea on the cape / where often my head within the cavern / was struck and sprayed by blows of the south wind" (1455-57). Here an image of nature in its violence is also one of fruitful cooperation between male and female forces that benignly companion rather than assault Philoktetes. Like his other final invocations of the landscape, it reflects a perspective entirely changed by the words of Herakles to which he has assented.

HERAKLES AND THE ENDING

Herakles brings about Philoktetes' salvation, altering the play's apparent *dénouement* and bringing its ending into conformity with the standard myth, according to which, as Sophokles' original audience would have known, Philoktetes *did* go to Troy, where he killed Paris and participated in the sack of the city, before returning home to Malis. The *deus ex machina* ending has had a mixed response from ancient and modern interpreters. Some find it psychologically impossible that Philoktetes, given his characterization throughout the play, should give in so readily. They dismiss the scene with Herakles as an arbitrary, purely theatrical conclusion that is not to be taken seriously. Others argue that Herakles' intervention is appropriate. For these interpreters, his special relationship to Philoktetes and the importance throughout the play of his bow, his previous sack of Troy (1439-40), and his apotheosis (726-29, 801-3) outweigh what they see as the psychological implausibility of Philoktetes changing his mind. Still others consider the apparent incommensurability of the "happy ending" with the rest of the play as a meaningful absurdity, a generic marker of a new kind of drama, a tragicomedy or romance, like Euripides' roughly contemporaneous dramas of intrigue and salvation: *Ion, Helen*, and *Iphigeneia among the Taurians*.

A lot depends on the assumptions one brings, and thinks Sophokles' original audience would have brought, to the play. Bernard Knox argues that *Philoktetes* is the one extant Sophoklean play in which "we...*want* [the hero] to give in, for this is the only way his terrible sickness can be healed. The drama of the assaults on the hero's will and his refusal to surrender is this time played out against a new background, the inevitability—more, the desirability—of his surrender."[26] On the other hand, while the intervention of Herakles may lead to Philoktetes' salvation, it does so by removing the circumstances that called forth his defining integrity and identity. When he leaves the island, Philoktetes relinquishes this identity by also leaving behind the necessity, and thus the opportunity, for his distinctive kind of heroic greatness.

Nevertheless, it is highly satisfying that Herakles provides Philoktetes with a way out of his self-defeating savagery and unproductive isolation. He can reach Philoktetes in a way that Neoptolemos cannot, because he appeals to him in the name of their old friendship, as well as on the authority of Zeus. "I've come for your sake," he tells him at 1413, using a word, *charin* ("sake"), that can mean both a spontaneously offered favor and the thanks that one gives in return for a favor received, as well as a disposition or attitude that evokes a favor or thanks from someone else. In 1413 *charin* suggests the favor that Philoktetes did Herakles by lighting his funeral pyre, relieving his suffering, and helping him to become a god—the favor for which Philoktetes had long ago received Herakles' unconquerable weapons (801-2). Herakles' appeal to Philoktetes to hear and obey his "authoritative words" (1417) and Philoktetes' agreement to do so are felt as reciprocal favors that continue their earlier relation of friendship.

---

[26] Knox, p. 117.

Herakles further strengthens this special relationship by offering himself as a role model for Philoktetes (1418-22):

> First of all, I'll tell you of my fortunes,
> how many labors I went through and labored at
> to win undying glory, as you can see.
> Be certain that to you too it is owed to suffer this—
> to make your life glorious after and through these labors.

A few lines earlier Philoktetes had told Neoptolemos, "Let me suffer what I must suffer" (1397), meaning, in Neoptolemos' words, "to go on living as you've been living, without salvation" (1396). Herakles in effect expands and transforms the notion of "what I must suffer" and brings about the "salvation" that had seemed impossible. This turns out to include not only getting off the island and returning home—certainly an improvement of his situation, but one that would leave Philoktetes just as socially unproductive as he is on Lemnos—but also a journey to Troy, where he will be cured of his painful disease and judged first in the army in bravery, killing Paris, sacking the city, and bringing home the "greatest prize for valor" (1423-29). "Since," says Herakles, "it is destined that the city be taken a second time / by my bow" (1439-40).

It has been suggested that Herakles' words in 1422, "to make your life glorious after and through these labors," following his mention of his own "undying glory" (1420), allude to a fifth-century hero cult in which Philoktetes was worshipped on Chrysê.[27] As I said in my Introduction (above, p. 00), hero cults constituted a kind of posthumous immortality for mortals whose actions and achievements during their lifetimes were so extraordinary that they seemed to transcend the normal limits of what human beings are capable of doing or suffering. A figure like this may have seemed repellent, even monstrous, when alive, but after death his

---

[27] S.J. Harrison, "Sophocles and the Cult of Philoctetes," *Journal of Hellenic Studies* 109 (1989), pp. 173-75. Philoktetes cerainly was worshiped in a hero cult at the supposed site of his grave in Makalla or on the Sybaris River, in the foot of Italy, but as Harrison says (p. 174), it is unclear whether Sophocles would have made, or his audience would have recognized, an allusion to this relatively obscure and distant cult, as opposed to one on an island near Lemnos, with which they would undoubtedly have been familiar. Appian, a second-century C.E. historian, mentions that the Roman general Lucullus in 73 B.C.E. overtook enemy forces "at a deserted island in the region of Lemnos, where there is displayed an altar to Philoktetes and, all in bronze, a serpent and a bow and a corslet bound with ribbons, a memorial to his suffering," (Appian, *Mithradates* 77, tr. Harrison).

or her power was socially harnessed, so to speak, at the site of the grave, where the "hero," as the cult-figure was called, could exert beneficent power on behalf of the local community of worshippers. Such cults are actually established as part of the dramatic action in *Ajax* and *Oidipous at Kolonos*, and the ending of *The Women of Trachis* may hint at a future cult of Herakles and his apotheosis on Mt. Oita.

Unlike the central figures of those plays, Philoktetes does not die and have his tomb consecrated as a site of power and a place of worship. Rather, Herakles refers to the glory that Philoktetes will "suffer" while alive, not after his death—the life he will make glorious by a wide range of heroic achievements, including both the "Iliadic" slaying of Paris and sacking of Troy and the "Odyssean" return home with the army's greatest prize of valor. To be sure, one might argue that because Philoktetes is symbolically dead when he is on Lemnos (cf. 946, 1018, 1030) and dislocated from his true self, the "life of glory" that Herakles speaks of should be thought of as posthumous. There is, however, a crucial difference between symbolic and actual death: hero cult can result only from the latter, and only when it is followed by appropriate offerings at the grave. *Philoktetes* reworks many themes also found in the earlier *Ajax* and later *Oidipous at Kolonos*, but it differs from those plays, as romance differs from tragedy, in large part because the hero does not die but is redeemed in his lifetime and restored to socially meaningful health and productivity.

Herakles is absolutely critical to the play's romance-ending: only he can intervene with both divine and human authority as the mouthpiece of Zeus and the friend of Philoktetes. Furthermore, it is likely that an Athenian audience would have been prepared to accept his appearance *ex machina* as ethically and dramatically appropriate not only because of these considerations, but because of his worship in Attic cults as a hero who "wards off harm" (*alexikakos*) and his legendary acceptance into the Eleusinian mysteries. There is no evidence of a late fifth-century cult of Herakles the Savior (*Hêraklês Sôtêr*) at Athens as there is at Thasos and Miletos, but it is possible that Athenian relations with these places would have made such a cult-identity familiar to Sophokles' original audience. If so, the intervention of Herakles to save both Philoktetes and the traditional story of the end of the Trojan War might have seemed to them especially fitting.

At the same time, Herakles' epiphany and his authoritative words about Zeus' plans for Philoktetes and the "life of glory" it is "owed [to him] to suffer" do not completely cancel Odysseus' opportunistic success in getting what he wanted all along. Herakles never mentions Odysseus, who is absent during the final scene. Nevertheless, as I have suggested (above, p. 101), audiences and readers would recall that it was his politically motivated intrigue that led to Philoktetes' salvation, and that in the *Odyssey* and the mythological tradition generally the chief credit for capturing Troy belonged to Odysseus, "the sacker of cities."

Neoptolemos' intertextual association in 1436-37 with the Odysseus of *Iliad* 10 and the allusion to his impiety during the sack of Troy (1440-44) open up confusing problems of interpretation, just as the action of the play seems to be shutting them down as part of its happy, romance ending. In addition, it is difficult, to be certain what Sophokles' original audience would have made of Herakles: whether the opportunity he affords Philoktetes' for socially relevant heroism through a return to the army at Troy and the war effort—the traditional mythological course of events—might not have seemed, in the twenty-second year of the Peloponnesian War, just as unrealistic or absurd as the ending of Euripides' *Orestes*, produced a year later, where Apollo intervenes to reverse an apparently irreversible dramatic action and restores all the characters to their traditional mythological destinies. Sophokles manages to balance the heroic, political, and generic complexities of his play in a way that would have left many in his audience, as it still leaves modern readers, divided in their responses, uncertain of their moral bearings, and challenged to think things through for themselves.

Presumably every viewer and reader of the play, from its first production to the present day, must decide for himself or herself which ending would be more compelling and satisfying: that Philoktetes stay on the island, that he go home with Neoptolemos and fight the Greeks if they come for him, or that he go to Troy to be healed and become a warrior-hero. When I first read *Philoktetes* as an undergraduate, I thought it was unfair that the hero had to leave the island and rejoin the Greek army. This seemed to me a defeat, a loss of the distinctive integrity and identity that were grounded in his isolation, endurance, and intransigence. Over the years, however, I have come to see Philoktetes' choice to leave in order to help sack Troy as courageous and triumphant rather than a defeat. It is no accident or anomaly that the Chorus, in the final words of the play, call on the sea nymphs "to come as saviors of a return home." For Philoktetes, a "return home" to Troy, where, paradoxically, he had never actually been, is a return home to the heroic self from which he had been dislocated by his disease and subsequent abandonment, an opportunity "to make [his] life glorious after and through these labors" (1422).

The intervention of Herakles and the known continuation of Philoktetes' story suggest the possibility of a heroic integrity and identity that transcend the various endings of the play that seem possible up to line

1408. The *deus ex machina* ending does not merely undermine or explode the actions and values of the play, as do apparently similar endings in Euripidean drama. Rather, without simplifying the complexities and costs of Philoktetes' possible choices and courses of action, it challenges audiences and readers (as it challenges Philoktetes himself) to rethink the world they live in, the moral choices they themselves are called on to make, and what is and is not ethically and politically desirable.

Appendix

Dio Chrysostom, *Discourse 52:*
Philoctetes in the Tragedians

Translated by D.A. Russell

I got up about an hour after daybreak, partly because I was unwell, and partly because the dawn air was cooler—more like autumn, though it was the middle of the summer. I attended to my toilet and said my prayers. Then I got into the carriage and took a number of turns on the racecourse, driving as gently and quietly as possible. I followed this up with a walk and a little rest; then I oiled myself and bathed and after a light meal began to read tragedies. They were all treatments of a single subject by the three great names, Aeschylus, Sophocles, and Euripides: the theft—or perhaps one should say violent robbery—of Philoctetes' bow. Anyway, Philoctetes is deprived of his weapon by Odysseus and himself taken to Troy, to a certain extent voluntarily, but with a degree of compulsion about it too, because he had been deprived of the weapon that gave him his livelihood on the island and confidence to face his disease, apart from being his claim to fame. I feasted on the performance, and reflected that if I had lived in Athens in those days I should not have been able to participate in a competition between these writers. Some indeed were present at competitions between the young Sophocles and the old Aeschylus, and again between Sophocles in his latter days and the young Euripides; but Euripides was altogether too late to encounter Aeschylus.

Moreover they rarely if ever competed with plays on the same theme. So I thought I was much indulged, and had discovered a new way of consoling myself for being ill. I produced the plays for myself (in my mind's eye) very splendidly, and tried to give them my whole attention,

*   *Ancient Literary Criticism*, ed. D.A. Russell and M. Winterbottom (Oxford, 1972), pp. 504-7. Reprinted by permission of Oxford University Press.

like a judge of the first tragic choruses. But had I been on oath, I could never have come to a decision. So far as I was concerned, none of them could have been beaten.

Aeschylus' grandeur and archaic splendour, and the originality of his thought and expression, seemed appropriate to tragedy and the antique manners of the heroes; it had nothing subtle, nothing facile, nothing undignified. Even his Odysseus, though shrewd and crafty for the times, was miles away from present-day standards of malevolence. He would seem an old-fashioned fellow indeed by the side of those who in our age claim to be simple and magnanimous. He did not need Athena to disguise him in order to prevent him from being recognized by Philoctetes, as Homer and (after him) Euripides have it. A hostile critic might perhaps say that Aeschylus was not concerned to make Philoctetes' failure to recognize Odysseus plausible. There is a possible defence, I think, against such an objection. The time was indeed perhaps not long enough for the features to fail to come to mind after a lapse of only ten years, but Philoctetes' illness and incapacity and the solitary life he had led so long also contribute to make the situation possible. People have suffered such a failure of memory as a result of illness or misfortune.

Nor did Aeschylus' chorus need to apologize, like that of Euripides. Both made up their choruses of inhabitants of Lemnos, but Euripides began by making them apologize for their neglect in not having come to see Philoctetes or given him any help for so many years, while Aeschylus simply brought the chorus on without comment. This is altogether simpler and more tragic, in contrast with Euripides' more sophisticated and painstaking treatment. If it had been possible to avoid every irrationality in tragedy, it might have been reasonable not to let this one pass either; but in fact poets often, for example, represent heralds as making several days' journey in one day. Secondly, it simply wasn't possible for none of the inhabitants of Lemnos to have approached Philoctetes or taken care of him. He could never have survived ten years without help. Probably therefore he did get some, but rarely and not on any grand scale, and no one chose to receive him in their house and nurse him because of the unpleasant nature of his illness. Indeed Euripides himself introduces one Actor, a Lemnian, who visits Philoctetes as an acquaintance who has often met him. Nor do I think it right to find fault with Aeschylus' making Philoctetes relate to an apparently ignorant chorus his desertion by the Achaeans and his whole history. The unfortunate often recall their troubles and weary their listeners, who know it all well and don't want to hear it again, with their perpetual narrations. Again, Odysseus' deception of Philoctetes and the arguments by which he wins him are not only more respectable—suitable to a hero, not a Eurybatus or a Pataecion[1]—but also, as it seems to me, more convincing. What was the need of elaborate art and guile in dealing with a sick man—and an archer too, whose prowess was useless the moment one came near him? To relate the disasters of the Achaeans, the death of Agamemnon, the death of Odysseus for a shocking crime, and total destruction of the army, was not only useful for cheering up Philoctetes and making him more willing to accept Odysseus' company, but also not implausible in view of the length of the campaign and the recent events consequent on the anger of Achilles, when Hector came near to burning the fleet.

Euripides' intelligence and care for every detail—nothing unconvincing or negligent is allowed to pass, and instead of bare facts he gives us the whole force of his eloquence—is the opposite of Aeschylus' simplicity. This is the style of the man of affairs and the orator; the reader can learn many valuable lessons from it. For example, Odysseus in the prologue is represented as revolving in his mind many rhetorically effective (*politika*) thoughts. He wonders about his own position. May he perhaps appear wise and intelligent to many people but in fact be the opposite? He could be living a secure, untroubled life—and here he is voluntarily involved in affairs and dangers! The cause, he says, is the ambition of talented and noble men; it is because they want reputation and fame among all mankind that they voluntarily undertake great and arduous tasks:

Nothing so vain as man was ever born.

Then he clearly and accurately explains the plot of the play, and why he has come to Lemnos. Athena has disguised him so that he shall not be recognized by Philoctetes when he meets him. (This is an imitation of Homer, who makes Athena disguise Odysseus when he meets various people such as Eumaeus and Penelope).[2] He says an embassy is going to come from the Trojans to Philoctetes, to offer him the kingdom of Troy in exchange for his own services and those of his bow. This complicates the story, and affords a starting-point for a speech in which he shows himself resourceful and eloquent enough to stand comparison with anyone in developing the opposite position. Nor does he make Odysseus come alone; Diomedes is with him, another Homeric touch. In short, he shows throughout the play great intelligence and convincingness in incident, and wonderful, hardly credible, skill of language. The iambics are clear, natural, rhetorically effective. The lyrics afford not only pleasure but many exhortations to virtue.

---

[1] Proverbial rogues; cf. Aeschines 3.137, 189; Plato, *Protagoras* 327d

[2] Cf. *Odyssey* 13.429ff., 16.172ff.

Sophocles comes between the two. He possesses neither Aeschylus' originality and simplicity, nor the craftsmanship, shrewdness, and rhetorical effectiveness of Euripides. His verse is dignified and grand, tragic and euphonious to the highest degree, combining great charm with sublimity and dignity. At the same time, his management of the story is excellent and convincing. He makes Odysseus arrive with Neoptolemus because it was ordained that Troy should be captured by Neoptolemus and Philoctetes with the bow of Heracles, but conceals himself while sending Neoptolemus to Philoctetes, telling him what he must do. Moreover the chorus is made up not, as in Aeschylus and Euripides, of natives, but of the crew of Odysseus' and Neoptolemus' ship. The characters are wonderfully dignified and gentlemanly. Odysseus is much gentler and more straightforward than in Euripides, Neoptolemus is simple and noble to excess, unwilling to win his point over Philoctetes by guile and deceit, but insisting on strength and openness, and afterwards, when Odysseus has persuaded him and he has deceived Philoctetes and got possession of the bow, unable to endure his victim's complaints and demands, and quite capable of giving him the bow back, despite Odysseus' appearance and attempt to stop him. Indeed, he does give it back in the end; and having done so then tries to persuade Philoctetes to go with him voluntarily to Troy. Philoctetes refuses to give way or comply, but begs Neoptolemus to take him home to Greece, as he had promised. The young man agrees and is ready to perform his promise, until Heracles appears and persuades Philoctetes to sail to Troy voluntarily. The lyrics are without the general reflections and exhortations to virtue which we saw in Euripides, but they possess extraordinary charm (*hêdonê*) and grandeur (*megaloprepeia*). It was not without cause that Aristophanes wrote:

He licked the lip of the jar, as it were, of honey-covered Sophocles.[3]

---

[3]   Fragment 581 Hall and Geldart

Suggestions for Further Reading

Historical and Cultural Background

Buxton, R. *Imaginary Greece: The Contexts of Mythology* (Cambridge, 1994)

Davies, J.K. *Democracy and Classical Greece*, 2nd edition (Cambridge, Mass., 1993)

Gantz, T. *Early Greek Myth: a Guide to Literary and Artistic Sources* (Baltimore and London, 1993)

Guthrie, W.K.C. "The World of the Sophists," *A History of Greek Philosophy*, Vol. 3 (Cambridge, 1969), pp. 1-319

Hornblower, S. *The Greek World, 479-323 B.C.* (London and New York, 1983)

Kerferd, G.B. *The Sophistic Movement* (Cambridge, 1981)

Parker, R. *Athenian Religion: A History* (Oxford, 1966)

Strauss, B. *Fathers and Sons in Athens: Ideology and Society in the Era of the* Peloponnesian War (Princeton, 1993)

Tyrrell, W.B. and F.S. Brown. *Athenian Myths and Institutions* (Oxford, 1991)

Williams, B. *Shame and Necessity* (Berkeley and Los Angeles, 1993)

Worman, N. *The Cast of Character: Style in Greek Literature* (Austin, 2002)

Works on Attic Tragedy
(most include some discussion of *Philoktetes*)

Bacon, Helen H. "The Chorus in Greek Life and Drama," *Arion*, 3rd Series, 3 (1994-95), pp.6-25

_____ "Aeschylus," *Ancient Writers: Greece and Rome*, Vol. 1, ed. T.J. Luce (New York, 1982), pp. 99-155, esp. 99-104 ("Aeschylus and Early Tragedy"), 104-8 ("Conventions of Choral Tragedy"), 108-14 "Tragic Story and Tragic Chorus)

Csapo, E. and W.J. Slater. *The Context of Ancient Drama* (Ann Arbor, 1995

Easterling, P.E. (ed.). *The Cambridge Companion to Greek Tragedy* (Cambridge, 1996

Goldhill, S. *Reading Greek Tragedy* (Cambridge, 1986)

Green, J.R. *Theatre in Ancient Greek Society* (London, 1994)

Hornblower, S. and A. Spawforth (eds.). *The Oxford Classical Dictionary*, 3rd Edition (Oxford, 1996): "theatre staging, Greek" by J.R. Green, pp. 1493-94; "tragedy, Greek" by R.A.S. Seaford and P.E. Easterling, pp. 1538-43

Jones, J. *On Aristotle and Greek Tragedy* (London, 1962)

Lesky, A. *Greek Tragic Poetry*, tr. M. Dillon (New Haven, 1983)

Rehm, R. *The Play of Space: Spatial Transformation in Greek Tragedy* (Princeton and Oxford, 2002)

_____ *Greek Tragic Theater*, rev. ed. (London, 1994)

Taplin, O. *Greek Tragedy in Action* (Berkeley, Los Angeles and London, 1978)

Vernant, J.-P. and P. Vidal-Naquet, *Myth and Tragedy in Ancient Greece*, tr. J. Lloyd (New York, 1988)

Vickers, B. *Towards Greek Tragedy* (London, 1973)

Wiles, D. *Tragedy in Athens: Performance Space and Theatrical Meaning* (Cambridge, 1997)

Winkler, J. and F. Zeitlin (eds.). *Nothing to Do with Dionysus?* (Princeton, 1990)

Worman, N. "Odysseus *Panourgos*: The Liar's Style in Tragedy and Oratory," *Helios* 26 (1999), 35-68

General Works on Sophokles
(including some discussion of *Philoktetes*)

Blundell, M.W. *Helping Friends and Harming Enemies: A Study in Sophoclean and Greek Ethics* (Cambridge, 1989)

Gellie, G.H. *Sophocles: A Reading* (Melbourne, 1972)

Kirkwood, G.M. *A Study of Sophoclean Drama* (Ithaca, 1958)

Knox, B.M.W. *The Heroic Temper: Studies in Sophoclean Tragedy* (Berkeley and Los Angeles, 1964)

Reinhardt, K. *Sophocles*, tr. H. and D. Harvey (Oxford, 1979)

Scodel, R. *Sophocles* (Boston, 1984)

Seale, D. *Vision and Stagecraft in Sophocles* (London, 1982)

Segal, C.P. *Sophocles' Tragic World: Divinity, Nature, Society* (Cambridge, Mass.,1995)

_____ "Sophocles," *Ancient Writers: Greece and Rome*, Vol. 1, ed. T.J. Luce (New York, 1982), pp. 179-207

_____ *Tragedy and Civilization: An Interpretation of Sophocles* (Cambridge, Mass., 1981)

Whitman, C.H. *Sophocles: A Study in Heroic Humanism* (Cambridge, Mass., 1951)

Winnington-Ingram, R.P. *Sophocles: An Interpretation* (Cambridge, 1980)

Works on *Philoktetes*

Avery, H.C. " One Ship or Two at Lemnos?" *Classical Philology* 97 (2002), pp. 1-20

_____ "Heracles, Philoctetes, Neoptolemus," *Hermes* 93 (1965), pp. 279-97

Belfiore, E. "*Xenia* in Sophocles' *Philoctetes*," *The Classical Journal* 89 (1994), pp. 113-29

Blundell, M.W. "The *Phusis* of Neoptolemus in Sophocles' *Philoctetes*," in *Greek Tragedy*, ed. I McAuslan and P. Walcot (Oxford, 1993), pp. 104-15

_____ "The Moral Character of Odysseus in *Philoctetes*," *Greek, Roman and Byzantine Studies* 28 (1987), pp. 307-29

Easterling, P.E. "Sophocles' *Philoctetes* and Modern Criticism," *Illinois Classical Studies* 3 (1978), pp. 27-39

Greengard, C. *Theatre in Crisis: Sophocles' Reconstruction of Genre and Politics in Philoctetes* (Amsterdam, 1987)

Hoppin, M.C. "Metrical Effects, Dramatic illusion, and the Two Endings of Sophocles' *Philoctetes*," *Arethusa* 23 (1990), 141-82

Kirkwood, G.M. "Persuasion and Allusion in Sophocles' 'Philoctetes', *Hermes* 122 (1994), pp. 425-36

Kitto, H.D.F. "Philoctetes," in *Form and Meaning in Drama* (London, 1956), pp. 87-137

Mandel, O. *Philoctetes and the Fall of Troy: Plays, Documents, Iconography, Interpretations* (Lincoln and London, 1981)

Milani, L.A. *Il mito di Filottete nella letteratura classica e nell'arte figurata* (Florence, 1879)

Rose, P.W. "Sophokles' *Philoktetes* and the Teachings of the Sophists," in *Sons of the Gods, Children of Earth: Ideology and Literary Form in Ancient Greece* (Ithaca, 1992), pp. 266-330

Schein, S.L. "Odysseus and the Language of Violence in Sophokles' Philoktetes," *Studi italiani di filologia classica* 20 (2002), pp. 45-49

_____"Herakles and the Ending of Sophokles' *Philoktetes*," *Studi italiani di filologia classica* 19 (2001), pp. 38-52

_____ "The Chorus in Sophocles' *Philoktetes*," *Studi italiani di filologia classica* 6 (1988), pp. 196-204

Scheliha, Renata von. *Der Philoktet des Sophokles: Ein Beitrag zur Interpretation der griechischen Ethos* (Amsterdam, 1970)

Taplin, O. "The Mapping of Sophocles' *Philoctetes*," *Bulletin of the Institute of Classical Studies in London* 34 (1988), pp. 69-77

_____ "Significant Actions in Sophocles' *Philoctetes*," *Greek, Roman and Byzantine Studies* 12 (1971), pp. 25-44

Worman, N. "Infection in the Sentence: The Discourse of Disease in Sophocles' *Philoctetes*," *Arethusa* 33 (2000), pp. 1-36